DATE DUE

JE 11'01			
AP 16 02			
DE 8 09			

DEMCO 38-296

REGIONS AND THE WORLD ECONOMY

REGIONS AND THE WORLD ECONOMY

*The Coming Shape of Global Production,
Competition, and Political Order*

ALLEN J. SCOTT

OXFORD UNIVERSITY PRESS · OXFORD
1998

...arendon Street, Oxford OX2 6DP

...ew York

...gota Bombay Buenos Aires

...Delhi Florence Hong Kong Istanbul

...Madrid Melbourne Mexico City

Nairobi Paris Singapore Taipei Tokyo Toronto Warsaw
and associated companies in
Berlin Ibadan

Oxford is a trade mark of Oxford University Press

Published in the United States
by Oxford University Press Inc., New York

© Allen J. Scott 1998

The moral rights of the author have been asserted

British Library Cataloguing in Publication Data
Data available

Library of Congress Cataloging in Publication Data
Scott, Allen John.
Regions and the world economy : the coming shape of global
production, competition, and political order / Allen J. Scott.
p.   cm.
Includes bibliographical references (p.).
1. Economic geography. 2. Regional economics. 3. International
economic relations. 4. Competition, International. I. Title.
HF1025.S364   1998
330.9—dc21
97–42645
CIP

ISBN 0–19–829405–0

1 3 5 7 9 10 8 6 4 2

Typeset by Graphicraft Typesetters Ltd., Hong Kong
Printed in Great Britain
on acid-free paper by
Biddles Ltd., Guildford & King's Lynn

ACKNOWLEDGEMENTS

I wish to thank John Agnew, Nicholas Entrikin, and Michael Keating for their helpful criticisms of an early draft of this book.

CONTENTS

List of Illustrations   ix

List of Tables   xi

1 Regions and the World Economy   1

2 The National Economy and the Sovereign State   9
    Geographic Frameworks of Economic and Political
      Order   9
    The Sovereign Territorial State   11
    Economy, State, Territory   13
    Beyond Fordism; Toward Globalism   20

3 The Coming Break-up of National Economies?   25
    A World of National Economies   25
    From Internationalization to Globalization:
      The Post-War Period   27
    The Geography of Globalization   42

4 The Global Mosaic of Regional Economies   47
    Contours of the Global Mosaic   48
    Forms of Regional Development   63
    The New World Map of Regions   68
    The Social Order of the Mosaic   71

5 The Regional Foundations of Economic Performance   75
    Industrial Organization and Economic Space   76
    The General Theory of Location   85
    The Specific Theory of Locational Agglomeration   91
    A Historical Geographic Perspective   98

6 Collective Order and Regional Development: Social and
    Cultural Regulation of Local Economic Systems   101
    The Regulatory Imperative   101
    A Backward Glance   104
    Socio-Cultural Regulation and Regional Strategic
      Choice   107
    Strategies of Regional Development   116

7 Prospects for Poor Regions 121
    The End of the Third World? 121
    Industrialization, Urbanization, and Development 124
    Region-Based Approaches to Economic Development 133

8 A World of Regions 137
    New Political Spaces 137
    Regional Directorates of the Twenty-First Century? 142
    Community, Local Democracy, and Citizenship 152

9 The Changing Geopolitics of Production, Competition, and Regional Interdependence 159

Index 165

LIST OF ILLUSTRATIONS

3.1 GDP and merchandise/service exports and imports for OECD countries, 1960–1994   30

3.2 US exports and imports as a percentage of gross domestic product, 1950–1994   31

3.3 Foreign trade as a percentage of gross domestic product in relation to gross domestic product for OECD countries, 1994   32

4.1 Current world distribution of metropolitan areas with populations greater than 1 million, 1994   50

4.2 A schematic representation of the contemporary geography of global capitalism   69

5.1 A pyramid-like economic space   79

5.2 A diffuse economic space with vertical and horizontal linkages   80

5.3 A growing industrial complex with dynamic vertical disintegration   96

6.1 A prospective view of a regional household furniture manufacturing system together with an associated set of institutional infrastructures   118

8.1 Fragment of an emerging global hierarchy of economic and political relations   138

LIST OF TABLES

3.1 Regression analysis of the relations between trade, total GDP, and GDP per capita, OECD countries, 1960–1994   34

3.2 The top ten multinational corporations ranked by foreign assets, 1994   37

3.3 Direct investment position abroad together with annual outflows and inflows of foreign direct investments, OECD countries, 1981–1994   39

4.1 The number of large metropolitan areas in the world, 1950, 1970, and 1990   51

4.2 The fifteen largest metropolitan areas in the world, 1950, 1970, and 1990   52

4.3 Manufacturing employment and value added in the forty US metropolitan areas with a population of 1 million or more, 1992   55

4.4 Service industry receipts in the forty US metropolitan areas with a population of 1 million or more in 1992   56

4.5 Manufacturing employment in the forty US metropolitan areas with a population of 1 million or more in 1992, by two-digit sector   58

4.6 Summary results of logistic regression analysis of locational clustering in two-digit manufacturing sectors, and four-digit clothing industry sectors   60

5.1 Schematic locational outcomes resulting from the combination of spatially dependent transactions costs and externalities   87

7.1 Logistic regression analyses of the effects of GDP per capita and industrialization on the proportion of total population living in urban areas, 1994   126

7.2 The footwear industry cluster in and around Novo Hamburgo, Rio Grande do Sul, Brazil, 1991   132

1

Regions and the World Economy

One of the apparent paradoxes of social theory today is that, precisely when it is preoccupied by visions of a shrinking world and a new global order, it simultaneously proclaims the rediscovered significance of geography in the arrangement of human affairs. To be sure, some analysts, caught up in a wave of enthusiasm induced by the speed and extent of globalization, have asserted that the end of geography is nigh,[1] but, as I hope to demonstrate at length in the present volume, this prognosis is entirely premature.

The shrinking of the modern world is in fact the very reason why geography now assumes or re-assumes such enormous importance. It goes without saying that geography has always played a major role in shaping historical outcomes, if only in the most obvious sense that spatial separation and propinquity, or more generally distance effects, invariably exert a profound influence over the structuring of economic and social relationships. Today, a new version of this socio-spatial duality is coming into being, one that is global in its reach and meaning, yet is also expressed as a patchwork of highly individualized localities or places. In the present context, I refer to these localities or places by the generic term *region*, by which I mean a geographic area of subnational extent. As such, my usage of the term is consistent with its traditional meanings, and stands in sharp contradistinction to the usage that is made of it nowadays by some social scientists to designate an area of continental proportions. In addition, I will usually use the term to designate a geographic area characterized by some minimal level of metropolitan development together with an associated tract of hinterland, i.e. an area that functions as the common spatial framework of daily life for a definite group of people, and that contains a dense mix of socio-economic activities subject to centripetal or polarization forces. This new socio-spatial duality thus assumes in its most general form the contours of a mosaic of regions scattered across

---

[1] Cf. R. O'Brien, *Global Financial Integration: The End of Geography*, London: Pinter, 1992.

the globe. This mosaic can be mapped out in terms of a network of local economies forming an integrated or quasi-integrated world-wide system of production and trade. As a corollary, and in light of the compression of space–time relations that has also been occurring at an accelerating pace in recent years, each region's economic fortunes are at once threatened and potentiated by developments in all other regions around the world.

As laconic as this initial formulation may be, its outlines are repeatedly visible in the countless daily minutiae of current events. One particularly revealing example may be cited in a visit to California by the Malaysian Prime Minister, Dr Mahathir bin Mohamad, in January 1997. The purpose of the visit was to promote Malaysia's projected Multimedia Super Corridor, a multi-billion-dollar mega-project extending thirty miles southward from Kuala Lumpur to the new international airport, and containing the planned cities of Putrajaya, which will become Malaysia's new national administrative capital, and Cyberjaya, a projected high-technology industrial center.[2] Cyberjaya will be the home of an ultra-modern multimedia university, and it is envisioned that the city will eventually employ upward of 150,000 workers in hundreds of small information technology and multimedia firms. Once completed, the Multimedia Super Corridor will raise the Kuala Lumpur region, and Malaysia more generally, to the leading edge of the information age—no mean accomplishment, if it can be achieved, for a country that only a few decades ago was a resource-dependent colonial backwater. Significantly, Dr Mahathir circumvented official US channels and, in a sort of paradiplomatic offensive, addressed himself directly to high-technology and media business circles in California in what turned out to be a most persuasive effort to induce them to participate (both as principals and as partners of Malaysian firms) in the Super Corridor project.

What is remarkable about this project is first of all its visionary breadth and scale, combining as it does something of Brasilia, the Chinese special economic zones, and the Japanese Technopolis Program, and second the active political efforts that have run in parallel with the planning and design phase to elicit the participation of firms whose roots go deeply into other regions in other parts of the world. The Malaysian Prime Minister's visit to California can be seen as

---

[2] *An Invitation to Malaysia's Multimedia Super Corridor: Leading Asia's Information Age*, Kuala Lumpur: Multimedia Development Corporation, no date.

an effort to build a sort of inter-regional coalition combining the competitive advantages of Silicon Valley in information technology, of Hollywood in entertainment production values, and of Kuala Lumpur in cheap but skilled labor able to provide the cultural and linguistic sensitivities necessary for effective penetration of the immense but still largely latent information and entertainment markets spread out across the continental triangle whose apexes are represented by China, India, and the Middle East. Such a coalition, if it can be successfully brokered and brought to term, would clearly represent a virtually irresistible economic force in Asia and the Pacific Rim, not to mention the world at large.

Successful or not—and it need scarcely be emphasized that the entire project is fraught with major risks and pitfalls—both the Multimedia Super Corridor itself and the putative connections that its promoters are trying to establish with other regions on the other side of the Pacific Ocean (and eventually with Japan and Europe too) represent harbingers of things to come. In particular, they are a foretaste of some of the economic and political trends emerging in a global system that is inclined in significant ways to emerge as a single unit, yet is also locationally anchored in regional divisions of labor that, to ever-increasing degrees, cut indiscriminately across the existing pattern of sovereign states.

The social mechanisms underlying the genesis of this nexus of global–regional relationships are of great complexity, and they will be examined at length in Chapters 4, 5, and 6. For present purposes, however, they can be described in terms of two seemingly opposed but at the same time intertwined factors:

1. Extraordinary improvements of modern transportation and communication technologies have occurred over the last few decades and have brought every point on the globe into close contact with every other point.
2. Contrariwise, many kinds of social and economic transactions remain extremely problematical, in the sense that significant failures occur when attempts are made to execute them over extended distances; in these cases, the mutual proximity of all relevant parties is required for effective inter-linkage to be established.

Thus, on the one hand, the physical transportation of people and goods has become ever more rapid, ever more cheap, and ever more reliable. It is now commonplace, for example, for business managers to travel from London to New York to attend a meeting and then to return home on the same day; for American supermarkets to stock plain spring water bottled in France or Sweden, and for firms located in different continents to enter into just-in-time production agreements with one another. Equally, the new electronic communications technologies in widespread use today make it possible for unlimited quantities of information to circulate around the globe in a fraction of a second. The net result of these trends is that the world is indeed becoming smaller, while by the same token the exotic is virtually disappearing as a meaningful experiential category in contemporary life. In today's world, the proximate and the distant are almost equally familiar.

On the other hand, the same trends have not only *not* undermined the region as the basis of dense and many-sided human interactions (though they have greatly affected many of the qualitative attributes of those interactions), but in many respects have actually reinforced it. Above all, and in spite of the great spatial extension of markets occasioned by globalization, the locational structure of production and work still by and large resists any universal tendency to geographic entropy. On the contrary, because production and work depend upon myriad detailed exchanges, dealings, flows, and webs of association that cannot be sustained effectively over long distances, selected groups of firms and individuals persistently coalesce out on the landscape to form dense regional complexes of economic and social activity. This phenomenon is manifest in part in the continued rapid progress of urbanization throughout the world—although it certainly does not account for all of the dynamism and complexity that this process typically displays. The very existence of a dense and expanding global tissue of urban areas, together with the fact that the same areas now account for much of the world's economic activity and population, are affirmations of the continued stubborn gyration of daily life around the orbit of the local, even though we are simultaneously connected in multiple ways to a vastly wider field of geographic eventuation.

This doubly faceted trend, in which definite articulations of social phenomena keep on materializing at the global (or supra-state) level and at the local (or infra-state level) means that the sovereign state itself is under enormous stress. In the face of this trend, some analysts, most prominently Ohmae,[3] have predicted the imminent demise of the nation-state and the advent of a borderless world, though this judgement seems unduly precipitate in view of the continued robust presence of behemoths like the United States, Germany, Japan, China, or Brazil on the world stage. What does appear to be occurring at the present time is a certain dislocation of the bonds that have hitherto held national economies and sovereign states together as the twin economic and political facets of a single social reality, as represented by phenomena such as the *American* economy, the *British* economy, the *French* economy, and so on. If Ohmae's version of the withering away of the state is somewhat extreme, it remains an authentic though distorted reflection of some deep underlying currents, which among other things raise important new questions about the established relations between the state and the economy (are they necessary or merely contingent?) and prompt us to begin seriously to inquire if there might not be practical substitutes for the customary forms of national government that have been bequeathed to us from the seventeenth and eighteenth centuries. Not unrelatedly, a distinct blurring of the traditional division between the state and civil society also seems to be taking place at the present moment of history.

In fact, theorists of the Regulationist School have already broached a number of these matters in their studies of the institutional foundations of capitalism and in their claims about the necessary formation of collective governance mechanisms (or modes of social regulation) in capitalism.[4] While the Regulationists have not made any decisive attempt to conceptualize possible versions of capitalism and their governance structures in the absence of a classical state apparatus, they have proposed an analysis of the political relations of capitalism that does acknowledge the important role of alternative non-governmental or quasi-governmental forms of social management

[3] K. Ohmae, *The Borderless World: Power and Strategy in the Interlinked Economy*, New York: Harper Business, 1990; K. Ohmae, *The End of the Nation State*, New York: Free Press, 1995.

[4] M. Aglietta, *A Theory of Capitalist Regulation: The US Experience*, London: New Left Books, 1979; R. Boyer, *La Théorie de la Régulation: une Analyse Critique*, Paris: Editions La Découverte, 1986; A. Lipietz, 'New tendencies in the international division of labor: regimes of accumulation and modes of social regulation', pp. 16–40 in A. J. Scott and M. Storper (eds.), *Production, Work, Territory: The Geographic Anatomy of Industrial Capitalism*, Winchester, Mass.: Allen & Unwin, 1986.

such as contractual agreements, civil associations and organizations, norms and conventions, private–public partnerships, and so on. In many instances, these alternative approaches to practical governance spring out of civil society as spontaneous responses to the search for collective order, or as cultural accretions that in one way or another come to function (well or badly) as regulatory institutions of the economy. In any case, they help to sustain capitalism as a functioning social system that would rapidly implode if its sole operating principles were purely capitalistic, which is the same as saying that profitability criteria and price signals in decentralized markets provide neither the necessary nor the sufficient conditions for the social reproduction of capitalism as a going concern.

We shall see in more detail later in the discussion that the successful social reproduction of capitalism is also crucially dependent on a framework of political institutions that provide guarantees of legal authority, property rights, and social order, and that have the capacity to intervene remedially whenever the workings of the economic system threaten to subvert its continued viability (e.g. at times of deep economic recession, labor unrest, inflation, pervasive market failure, and so on). Moreover, as the sovereign state continues to lose ground before the partial reconstitution of capitalism at supra-state and infra-state levels, we can observe many of these alternative forms of governance starting to take shape at corresponding spatial levels. Concomitantly, many new notions about the nature of democracy and citizenship and their appropriate geographic frames of reference are now being thrust ever more forcefully into the limelight.

The chapters that follow seek to build upon and to amplify these peremptory remarks. My argument advances over three main fronts. First, I provide some extended historical and geographical documentation of the trends briefly alluded to above, with particular emphasis on a series of propositions about the coming partial break-up of national economies and their re-configuration in a global mosaic of regions. Second, I explore the theoretical underpinnings of these propositions by means of an inquiry into the locational dynamics of modern economic systems and their associated modes of social regulation. Third, I then describe some of the principal institutional transformations and innovations that are occurring in response to the underlying shifts that I maintain are occurring in the world's economic geography, and I offer a few remarks as to what they might mean for everyday political life in general. My overall claim is that we are currently experiencing a major geopolitical shift in conditions of production, competition, and interdependence involving an as yet uncompleted (indeed, incipient) transition from an international to a global economic system. The former can be described schematically as an old international regime rooted in a comparatively stable system of sovereign states, each with an internal hierarchy of more or less subservient local governments.[5] The latter is represented by a diffuse global order characterized by emerging and still primitive governance structures, and in which interrelations between states are in some degree giving way to interrelations between far-flung regional economies joined together in complex patterns of competition and collaboration, often accompanied by novel expressions of regional political self-assertion.

If true, this claim casts a new and important light on the economic geography of the modern world, just as it also poses urgent issues about appropriate forms of economic governance and political mobilization at all geographic scales as we move into the twenty-first century. In particular, it raises the burning question of how, in a prospective global mosaic of regional economies, individual regions can maximize their competitive advantages through intra-regional policy efforts while simultaneously working together collaboratively to create an effective world-wide inter-regional division of labor with appropriate built-in mechanisms of mutual aid, and especially with some modicum of collective assistance for failing or backward regions.

[5] M. Keating, *The Invention of Regions: Political Restructuring and Territorial Government in Western Europe*, Advanced Research on the Europeanisation of the Nation State, Working Paper no. 8, Oslo: Research Council of Norway, 1996.

2

The National Economy and
the Sovereign State

GEOGRAPHIC FRAMEWORKS OF ECONOMIC AND
POLITICAL ORDER

Throughout the history of capitalism, the institutionalized expression
of economic and political life has typically attained its highest and
clearest articulation in the national economy and the sovereign state,
respectively. Over the last couple of centuries, indeed, the relationship between the two has commonly been so strong and organic in
its nature that it tends to pass for a self-evident if not necessary condition. An important consequence of this notion of the national economy and the state as integrated social entities is that the international
system has often been understood as a disorderly field of competition
in which a finite number of these phenomena interact holistically with
one another rather like billiard balls in constant motion.[1] The concept
of the national economy, however, is under considerable pressure at
the present time in light of the fast-moving changes that have been
occurring world-wide in structures of economic and political interaction. More particularly, I see this pressure as pointing directly toward
the need for a reconceptualization of the economic and political geography of the modern world, with one of its main ingredients being an
effort to come to terms with the widening mismatch between the
sovereign state as a definite territorial unit and the realities of modern economic systems whose ever-extending and ramifying tentacles
now reach out across the world. I shall argue below that this intensifying geographic polymorphism of the economic order is presently
driving forward a corresponding but also reflexive transformation of
the political order such that the sovereignty of the state is beginning
to disintegrate at significant points of contact with the economic. As
Mann has shown, the state has never really been a coherent, unitary

[1] K. N. Waltz, *The Theory of International Politics*, Reading, Mass.: Addison-Wesley,
1979.

institution,[2] but now political and regulatory control is diffusing more than it ever has in the past away from the classical state apparatus and into other institutional repositories of collective decision-making and action.

As these processes run their course, a new fourfold spatial hierarchy of economic and political relationships seems to be taking shape. The different levels of the hierarchy may be briefly identified as follows:

1. the *global*, as constituted by rather disparate but rapidly materializing networks of economic activity (finance, trade, foreign direct investment, international joint ventures, and so on), partially but very imperfectly regulated by a system of international contractual regimes, understandings, and organizations;
2. the *plurinational*, as represented by a group of multination blocs, such the EU, NAFTA, ASEAN, APEC, CARICOM, and MERCOSUR, most of them as yet, with the exception of the EU, rather weakly developed;[3]
3. the *national*, focused on the classical sovereign state, though with a sort of hollowing-out process now distinctly beginning to erode elements of its economic and political integrity;
4. the *regional*, which is currently emerging, or re-emerging, as a vibrant but also extremely puzzling articulation of modern economic and political life.

The units identified in each of these four tiers represent complex spatial frameworks of investment, productive enterprise, market competition, and political regulation, and they all pose major analytical questions, both in their own right and in the ways in which they depend upon and constrain events in units at other levels in the hierarchy.

All of these levels, and their mutual interactions, play a critical role in the argument laid out in the present volume. The main discussion will concentrate on the two extremes of the hierarchy—the global and regional levels—though the intermediations between the two (which are increasingly direct) need always to be investigated against the background of the plurinational and the national. My argument expands at length on the proposition that a new global capitalist eco-

[2] M. Mann, *The Sources of Social Power*, II, *The Rise of Classes and Nation States, 1760–1914*, Cambridge: Cambridge University Press, 1993.

[3] H. Bourguinat, 'L'Émergence contemporain des zones et blocs régionaux', pp. 3–16 in J-L. Muchielli and F. Célimène (eds.), *Mondialisation et Régionalisation: un Défi pour l'Europe*, Paris: Economica, 1993.

nomy is coming into existence, with regions—as defined in Chapter 1—constituting the fundamental building blocks or motors of the entire system. As such, regions are also evolving as vital centers of economic regulation and political authority, and they are becoming, as a corollary, the basic framework for new kinds of social community and for new approaches to practical issues of citizenship and democracy.

In spite of these bold declarations, the sovereign state is still, without any question, the principal locus of power in today's world. Even though there has been some tendency toward a recomposition of this power at other levels of the hierarchy described above, the state remains by far the chief axis of economic and political organization within the hierarchy, and it retains a robust capacity to assert its influence over the logics that operate at all other levels. It is therefore in order that we begin with a brief discussion of the nature and historical emergence of the state, and of the forces that now seem to be encouraging the dissipation of certain elements of its power.

THE SOVEREIGN TERRITORIAL STATE

The origins of the modern state system lie roughly in the period extending from the Treaty of Westphalia, which ended the Thirty Years War in 1648, to the Congress of Vienna, which ended the Napoleonic Wars in 1815. This is a time that coincides not only with the formation of the sovereign state as the condensation and pinnacle of society as a whole, but also with the completion of the transition from feudalism to capitalism and the assimilation of the latter system into the corporate body of the nation and the state.

Three essential features mark the state as it emerges fully formed out of this period of gestation, and as it was theorized in its classical form by contemporary observers from Hobbes to Hegel:

1. Its realm extends over a definite territory, which among other things signifies that it possesses rights of eminent domain over the land and its resources.

2. This realm is populated by a citizenry which in many cases, but certainly not always, comes to see itself as a nation (an 'imagined community', to use Anderson's terminology[4]) within the state.

[4] B. Anderson, *Imagined Communities: Reflections on the Origins and Spread of Nationalism*, London: Verso, 1983.

3. The state is the ultimate authority on all political and legal matters; i.e., it constitutes an apparatus of governance regulating society as a whole, and possessing a monopoly of physical coercion wherever it meets with resistance to its mandates. In addition, the state reserves for itself the authority to tax and the final power to adjudicate property rights.

The rule and prerogatives of the state, however, no matter how absolutist a pose it may strike, are always subject to social contestation and redefinition in practice. Existing political arrangements are continually under stress internally as different social interests come into collision with one another, or as ascending factions of society stake their claims to a share in power. States are also constantly under threat externally from one another, particularly when one of them is inclined to expand at the expense of the others. By the same token, and in the absence of any legitimate overarching mechanism of international regulation, the sphere of inter-state relations becomes an unstable arena of shifting coalitions, interspersed with long-term rivalries and the occasional trauma of war. The logic of this situation, picking up on the billiard-ball analogy once again, has been characterized by Waltz as a condition of anarchy held in check only by temporary balances of power.[5]

The classical sovereign state, then, encompasses a specific territory inhabited by a citizenry that either actually or latently can be characterized as a nation, and it constitutes a durable but eventually transmutable authority that owes allegiance to no one but itself. It was within this frame of reference that the old feudal order saw its final burst of glory in the France of Louis XIV, that the progression to capitalism was worked out, and that full-blown industrial development was ushered in in different countries.[6] Capitalism itself came gradually into being over the seventeenth and eighteenth centuries in the steady though often troubled emergence of free markets in land and labor, the formation of effective institutions of monetary and financial order, and the consolidation of the mechanisms of capital accumulation.[7] In the historical unfolding of these events, the classical state in Western Europe was bit by bit—though never totally—colonized from within and below by the burgeoning social relationships of capitalism.

[5] Waltz, *International Politics*.

[6] P. Anderson, *Lineages of the Absolute State*, London: NLB, 1974.

[7] K. Polanyi, *The Great Transformation: The Political and Economic Origins of Our Time*, New York: Rinehart, 1944.

With the advancement of industrial capitalism over the nineteenth century, the relations between the national economy and the state on a finite geographical territory became ever more tightly bound together. This interpenetration occurred not only because of steady improvements in technologies of socio-spatial integration (ranging from the development of new transportation and communication systems to the deepening capacity of the state to monitor all manner of economic and social outcomes), but also because the state, through its custodianship of such basic apparatuses as the law, monetary and financial regulations, the educational system, and so on, became the essential guarantor of those institutional underpinnings without which markets cannot work, and which help to stabilize the numerous inner disequilibria and imbalances of capitalist society. Even at the height of putative *laisser-faire* capitalism, the spheres of economic and social life were everywhere shot through with political accommodations that provided the conditions of survival of the entire system, e.g. in such matters as the control of imports and exports, the surveillance of factory work conditions, urban planning, public health legislation, the formulation of company law, and so on. At the same time, early capitalism fostered the spread of liberal democratic ideals as a sort of political counterpart to the play of markets in the economic arena, and these ideals were widely put into practical effect. Capitalist society thus made its historical appearance as a system offering enormous flexibility and wide margins of manoeuver for economic and political action. For the most part, however, it was confined geographically by the boundaries of the territorial state, notwithstanding the fact that it was also marked from its inception by strong impulses to outward expansion.

ECONOMY, STATE, TERRITORY

The economic geography of early capitalism

Britain, of course, was in the vanguard of capitalist economic development, and its concomitant accumulation of wealth established it as the hegemonic power of the nineteenth century, with other countries of Western Europe and North America following closely on its heels.

In each country, manufacturing industry led the process of growth, though the specific character of industrialization differed in detail from case to case depending on such matters as resource availability, market structures, and rates of capital accumulation. In all instances, however, industrialization brought about massive reorganization of the internal space of each country by inducing concentrated clusters of development in some areas while leaving other areas virtually untouched. The result is that, from the earliest moments of capitalist development, an intra-national pattern of spatial unevenness has been clearly inscribed on the landscape.

Virtually everywhere, this unevenness can be identified in terms of a bipartite structure of core and peripheral spaces, analogous to the core–periphery layout that according to Wallerstein has been a chronic feature of historical capitalism at the world scale.[8] From the first, this core–periphery structure at the intra-national scale assumed the form of (*a*) a dominant heartland region or regions containing thriving industries and growing cities,[9] and (*b*) a residual peripheral area dominated by agricultural pursuits and punctuated by occasional resource extraction and service centers. In the United States, the primeval heartland of late eighteenth- and early nineteenth-century industrialization and urbanization comprised above all the North-east of the country, stretching westward from New England and New York and reaching eventually through the Great Lakes area to the Midwest. In Western Europe an analogous geographic complex could be found extending from the coalfield areas of Britain across much of the Northern European Plain with occasional outliers to the north and the south. This peculiar spatial pattern progressively took on clearer shape over much of the nineteenth century and continued to dominate the landscape of North American and Western European nations well into the twentieth century, just as Wallerstein's core–periphery scheme at the world scale is still discernible today within the complex palimpsest of global economic and political geography.

The reorganization of geographic space wrought by the early stirrings of capitalism can in part be understood in terms of the preordained and patently irregular distribution of physical resources and transport opportunities over the face of the earth. This investigative point of departure, however, can never fully explain the intensity of the variations in the types and density of development experienced at

---

[8] I. Wallerstein, *The Modern World System*, ii, *Mercantilism and the Consolidation of the European World Economy 1600–1750*, New York: Academic Press, 1980.

[9] A. F. Weber, *The Growth of Cities in the Nineteenth Century* (1899), Ithaca, NY: Cornell University Press, 1963.

different locations and in different countries in early capitalism. This is a complex question which will be taken up again in more detail in Chapter 5, but which in the context of the present historical discussion can be broached in a preliminary manner in terms of some eighteenth- and nineteenth-century debates on the division of labor (i.e. issues of the specialization and complementarity of production activities) and on international trade policy (i.e. questions about open markets versus protectionism).

At the end of the eighteenth century, Adam Smith had shown how the widening and deepening of the technical division of labor within the individual workshop depends upon periodic extensions of the market.[10] The greater the volume of output from any workshop, the more feasible it becomes to reorganize the internal structure of production by dividing the elements of what was formerly one worker's daily routine into a series of sub-tasks to be carried out by detail workers. As this process moves forward, production becomes increasingly streamlined and overall productivity tends to rise.

Smith's argument was focused on the individual workshop and its internal technical division of labor. The argument can be extended, however, to the social division of labor as represented by vertically disintegrated workshops in which specific kinds of task or groups of tasks spin off to become specialized production units in their own right. Where this occurs in such a way that a given sector, say textiles or clothing or metal-working, is becoming more and more partitioned into specialized but interlinked sub-sectors—thus creating what in modern parlance might be referred to as dense value-added networks—the result is often a massive trend to spatial agglomeration leading in turn to a considerable amplification of urban and regional growth patterns. Frequently, individual regions will then specialize in particular types of product and inter-regional trade will ensue.

The claim subsequently elaborated by Ricardo in the early nineteenth century, to the effect that countries (and by extension cities and regions) trade with one another on the basis of their comparative advantages in production, added a new and potent element to the analysis.[11] Ricardo showed that commodity exchanges between two

---

[10] A. Smith, *The Wealth of Nations* (1776), Harmondsworth, Middlesex: Penguin Books, 1970. See also G. J. Stigler, 'The division of labor is limited by the extent of the market', *Journal of Political Economy*, 69 (1951): 213–25.

[11] D. Ricardo, *Principles of Political Economy and Taxation* (1871), Harmondsworth, Middx: Penguin Books, 1971.

countries will often occur even though one of the countries may not enjoy an absolute cost advantage in any commodity that it produces. So long as the latter country has a simple *relative or comparative* cost advantage in relation to its prospective partner, trade can occur to the mutual benefit of both. In Ricardo's words,

it is this principle which determines that wine shall be made in France and Portugal, that corn shall be grown in America and Poland, and that hardware and other goods shall be manufactured in England.[12]

Above all, different countries, cities, and regions have distinctive kinds of factor endowments, and, as the standard Heckscher–Ohlin interpretation of Ricardian theory showed, divergences in relative scarcities of these endowments are apt to be manifest in efficient forms of local economic specialization and trade, provided that political frontiers do not disrupt underlying market mechanisms.[13] This therefore will heighten the spatial variegation of the economic landscape, while the deepening division of labor consequent upon enlarged markets will accentuate processes of economic growth and development in areas opening up to trade.

Both Smith and Ricardo used their analytical insights to argue forcefully for open markets and free trade as the essential prerequisites of economic development and growth, and their arguments encountered a receptive audience in Britain which, at the time they were writing, was in the throes of vigorous international economic expansion. In 1841, however, Friedrich List, arguing from the vantage point of a much less economically advanced Germany, suggested that free trade would in the long run lead to very unequal developmental outcomes between different countries depending on their relative levels of industrialization.[14] Free trade between Britain and Germany in particular was likely to work to the advantage of the former and to penalize the latter country. In view of Britain's earlier start down the pathway of industrial capitalism, free trade according to List would have opened Germany to a flood of British manufacturing goods, thereby nipping German industrialization in the bud. Corresponding increases in the

---

[12] Ricardo, *Principles of Political Economy and Taxation*, 152.

[13] E. F. Heckscher and B. Ohlin, *Heckscher–Ohlin Trade Theory*, trans., ed., and intro. by H. Flam and M. J. Flanders, Cambridge, Mass.: MIT Press, 1991.

[14] F. List, *National System of Political Economy* (1841), Fairfield, NJ: A. M. Kelley, 1977. See also D. Levi-Faur, 'Friedrich List and the political economy of the nation-state', *Review of International Political Economy*, 4 (1997): 154–78.

export of agricultural goods from Germany to Britain unquestionably would have raised overall German levels of prosperity, but could not be counted on to generate the same advantageous kinds of multiplier and externality effects as indigenous manufacturing industry. Among these effects we may count such phenomena as technological learning, the building of managerial and entrepreneurial cultures, the large-scale accumulation of physical capital, and so on. The evident deduction is that national policy (as represented, for example, by the high tariff barriers established by the Zollverein in the specific case of the German states) should therefore seek to protect infant industries, permitting them to evolve to the point where they can achieve proficiency in the organization of production processes and the design of products. Only at that stage would free trade begin to work to the long-run advantage of later industrializers like Germany.

As it turned out, this kind of protectionist policy served the purposes of German economic growth in the nineteenth century very well indeed, and in addition was a remarkable presentiment of the Japanese approach to industrial development later in the nineteenth century, and of certain features of East and South-east Asian industrialization in the second half of the twentieth. Although List's ideas have been much neglected in comparison with those of Smith and Ricardo, shadows of his important insights can be discerned in some versions of modern trade theory and economic growth theory, including, as we shall note in due course, regional development theory, where what we might provisionally call a neo-Listian approach has been gathering momentum in recent years.

In any case, and notwithstanding the influence of Smith and Ricardo, and the potent ideology of *laisser-faire*, nineteenth-century capitalism was pre-eminently a series of national concerns which entered the present century as a collection of distinctively American, British, French, etc. social formations. As such, it was encompassed within strong sovereign states, and was underpinned by a prevailing spirit of nationalism stamping each specific instance with an unambiguous social and political identity.

The high-water mark of national capitalism

In the early decades of the twentieth century, capitalism began to go through yet another of the major episodes of restructuring that periodically sweep across it, and was being reorganized along the lines that would define it over much of the rest of the century. These early decades were marked by the rise of mass-production industry, itself derivative from the massive internal economies of scale that flowed forth with the perfection of the moving-assembly-line and continuous-process technologies at the beginning of the century. Mass production in turn came to constitute the basis of the large multidivisional corporation.[15] Sectors such as cars, machinery, domestic appliances, steel, petroleum refining, and processed foods were all caught up in this transformation. Simultaneously, the principal assembly industries with their backward linkages extending through many tiers of input and service providers functioned as major growth poles in each national economy. The lead plants constituting these growth poles, together with large cohorts of upstream industries, then regularly re-appeared in locational form as massive spatial agglomerations of firms and workers. These agglomerations provided much of the economic and geographic backbone of large manufacturing cities in the period from about the 1920s to the 1960s, and underpinned their role as the dominant foci of growth in the national economies of both North America and Western Europe over the same period. Most of these cities were located in the core manufacturing belts or regions whose roots had already been established in individual countries in the previous century.

In parallel with the development of mass production and its embodiment in giant production units, a 'fordist' system of labor relations also came into being as one of the key social conditions of economic success. The primary characteristics of fordism as such can be described in terms of a bipartite division of the mass-production labor force into (*a*) a group of unskilled and semi-skilled blue-collar workers, assigned to routine jobs defined by the minute technical division of labor that was made possible by the moving assembly line, and (*b*) a cadre of highly skilled white-collar workers (managers, professionals, engineers, technicians, and so on), responsible for the overall organization of production, and above all charged with the task of continual refinement of production processes so as to reduce the discretionary decision-making power of blue-collar workers on the factory floor to the minimum. In addition, wherever fordism made its advent, one version or another of a set of contractual agreements between

---

[15] A. D. Chandler, *Strategy and Structure*, Cambridge, Mass.: MIT Press, 1962.

management and labor was invariably forthcoming in which the conditions of work, pay, benefits and entitlements, and collective bargaining were typically laid out in considerable detail.

In the United States these arrangements were formalized in the Wagner Act of 1935, which among other things made union organizing fully legal under certain specified conditions, and permitted the establishment of an orderly nation-wide system of collective bargaining. Mass production became the linchpin of the sustained prosperity of the United States and other advanced industrial societies over the 1950s and 1960s, and the fordist managerial structures and labor relations systems that were steadily built into it helped to safeguard that prosperity by securing the elements of a durable industrial peace.

Yet, one further major ingredient was needed in this powerful social mix before it could finally take off into sustained growth. Fordist mass production was subject to severe cyclical downturns, most clearly exemplified by the traumatic depression of the early 1930s. In the normal course of events, such downturns predictably sap away at the economic and social bases of the entire system by disrupting production, undermining confidence in the economy, and throwing workers into unemployment for prolonged periods of time.

In response to this problem, a series of governmental interventions was launched, starting hesitantly with Roosevelt's New Deal in the early 1930s, proceeding more resolutely through the immediate post-war years, and resulting by the late 1950s in the full-blown advent of keynesian welfare-statist national policy. Under the umbrella of this broad approach, national governments provided the macroeconomic conditions (deficit spending and demand stimulation) and the social guarantees (unemployment insurance and other welfare measures, including aid to lagging regions) that over the 1950s and 1960s kept the system from falling into protracted recession or exacerbated social conflict, and laid the conditions for the long post-war boom—what some authors have labelled the Golden Age of Capitalism.[16]

The period of the long boom, which finally came to an end only in the late 1960s and early 1970s, represents the zenith of the fordist mass-production system as a whole, and, concomitantly, of the

---

[16] See e.g. the collection of essays edited by S. A. Marglin and J. B. Schor, *The Golden Age of Capitalism*, Oxford: Clarendon Press, 1990. For a critique of the Golden Age thesis consult M. J. Webber and D. L. Rigby, *The Golden Age Illusion: Rethinking Post-war Capitalism*, New York: Guilford, 1996.

phenomenon of the national economy as a distinctive social structure. This is not to say that international economic activity was at a low ebb during the fordist epoch. On the contrary, and especially after World War 2, both international trade and foreign direct investments rose significantly as the domestic economies of the advanced capitalist countries expanded. But the same economies were fundamentally being driven forward by *national* fordist mass-production sectors or growth poles, together with the *national* policy frameworks providing critical coordination and steering functions.

The essentially national flavor of this economico-political conjuncture was given yet further emphasis by the tensions of the Cold War, and above all, in the United States, by the insistence of the federal government on maintaining a strong and self-reliant domestic economy. The Cold War was also an occasion for persistent and large-scale military spending, which, as it happens, fitted perfectly into this general scheme of things, for throughout the post-war decades it functioned as one of the privileged instruments of various governments in North America and Western Europe for putting keynesian policies into effect.

BEYOND FORDISM; TOWARD GLOBALISM

As the 1970s advanced, the fordist mass-production system was falling into crisis virtually everywhere. It faced both saturating markets and mounting challenges from Japanese manufacturers (soon to be joined in the competitive race by the newly industrializing countries), and as the problems of the production system deepened the keynesian welfare-statist regulatory framework itself seemed to become capable only of generating higher and higher levels of stagflation. Simultaneously, the old heartland regions that had constituted the locational foundations of fordist mass production in the advanced capitalist countries of North America and Western Europe lost much of their former dynamism and re-emerged as rustbelts, with new industrial investments shifting to other geographic areas. In the United States, the Carter presidency of 1976–9 represents the last trace of the old political order, and all the more so as any attempt at keynesian demand stimulation was now apt to result not in domestic growth but in rising floods of imports, thus aggravating the crisis.

Even as fordist mass production was starting to be pushed from center-stage in the major capitalist countries over the 1970s and early 1980s, burgeoning new sectors, often marked by drastically new forms of production organization, were moving into the economic vacuum that was being created. In the first place, the leading edges of capitalist development were now being increasingly identified with booming sectors such as (*a*) high-technology manufacturing, (*b*) consumer-oriented industries making everything from clothing to high-performance cars to films and television programs, and resolutely focused on niche markets, and (*c*) personal and business services. In the second place, these sectors were also the carriers of a rising new technological paradigm involving flexible forms of production based on electronic technologies and a resurgence of de-routinized work practices requiring high levels of human handicraft and discretionary performance.

These developments permitted radical shifts in output configurations, away from the standardization that was the rule under fordist mass production, and toward more customized, differentiated, and rapidly changing product designs. One effect of this change has been rising levels of entrepreneurialism and competitiveness within the post-fordist economic environment. Another has been a major revival of local economies on a quite different spatial and functional basis from the regional manufacturing systems that sustained fordist mass production. At the same time, the rise of thatcherism in Britain and of reaganism in the United States marked a decisive break with keynesian welfare-statism as an overarching system of political arrangements. In its place, a still-evolving neo-conservative political agenda was set in motion, with its central objectives firmly directed to the withdrawal of central government from heavy-handed economic management and, wherever possible, to the reprivatization of social services. Over the 1980s and 1990s, this agenda spread, in one version or another, to virtually all of the advanced capitalist societies.

These shifts in the economic and political complexion of capitalism after the crisis of the 1970s have been associated with two main lines of geographic change. On the one hand, an accelerating globalization of economic activity is currently in full swing, if only in the minimal sense that political, institutional, and geographic barriers to flows of goods, services, and investments over national boundaries are constantly receding so that these boundaries are now more porous than they have been for at least the past century. Albert and Brock have referred to this process as 'debordering', a term that succinctly denotes the opening up of given political territories and the increasing proclivity for economic activities to spill over beyond the political confines that had earlier exerted such severely restrictive effects.[17] On the other hand, a series of new industrial spaces and regions are rising to prominence in former peripheral areas which had earlier been passed over by the main currents of industrialization and which are now beginning to function as new engines of the global economy.[18]

With globalization, there has been a gradual evolution of the classical territorial state toward what Rosecrance initially referred to as the 'trading state', and then, in a more radical formulation, the 'virtual state'.[19] Additionally, with the wholesale resurgence of localized production systems, national economies are starting to look more and more like loose confederations of regional economies.[20] As problematical as these assertions may be at this stage of the discussion, they aptly point to the increasing disjunction between the narrow and static political territoriality of the state and the wider dynamic territoriality of the economy at the present time.

These circumstances seem to call into question the very concept— frequently taken as being self-evident—of a national economy and its identification with the sovereign state. Even if the continued existence of national monetary and fiscal systems means that it is still meaningful in certain senses to speak of national economic aggregates, what is important for our purposes is that *systems of production and exchange* are increasingly being reconfigured at geographic scales of operation other than the national. At the very least, given the accelerating shift of critical articulations of economic and political activity to both supra-national and infra-national levels, the specific connections between the economy and the state now appear more as a historical contingency than as a necessary and inviolable social bond.

To be sure, the sovereign state does not function solely as a regulator of economic affairs, but also has forceful social and cultural missions that are imbued with powerful meanings. The inertia of these

[17] M. Albert and L. Brock, 'Debordering the world of states: new spaces in international relations', *New Political Science*, 35 (1996): 69–106.

[18] A. J. Scott, *New Industrial Spaces: Flexible Production Organization and Regional Development in North America and Western Europe*, London: Pion, 1988.

[19] R. Rosecrance, *The Rise of the Trading State*, New York: Basic Books, 1986; R. Rosecrance, 'The rise of the virtual state', *Foreign Affairs*, 75 (1996): 45–61.

[20] R. M. Locke, 'The composite economy: local politics and industrial change in contemporary Italy', *Economy and Society*, 25 (1996): 483–510.

meanings will no doubt be sufficient to raise political impedances capable of slowing down further divergence between the domains of the economic and the classical state. It seems improbable, however, that they should permanently arrest the trends described. The same trends throw into sharp relief many difficult questions about the structure and logic of the political apparatuses that will undoubtedly materialize in extra-state contexts in response to the mounting regulatory tasks posed by the continued restructuring of capitalism at both the global and regional levels as we enter the twenty-first century.

3

The Coming Break-up of National Economies?

A WORLD OF NATIONAL ECONOMIES

In spite of the territorial boundaries historically imposed by the sovereign state on the organization of economic activity, capitalism, as we have seen, has always shown an urge to push out beyond the confines of the state in quest of new sources of raw materials, new reservoirs of labor, new investment opportunities, and new markets. The continual expansionary thrust of capitalism over the very long run makes it extremely mutable in geographic terms. Even as early as the eighteenth century an international network of trade had appeared under mercantilism, and as industrial capitalism took hold over the early nineteenth century world trade continued to grow. In 1830, total world exports represented 4.6% of world GDP; by the last two decades of the century, they were hovering at a level close to 11.0%.[1]

This disposition to extra-national economic linkage, however, in the past has typically been subservient to national interests, with major capitalist states pulling back into protectionism and autarchy whenever internationalization seemed to threaten them. Thus, in the twentieth century, in the period between the two world wars, international trade collapsed in the combined tensions created by a major economic depression and extreme political instability. Indeed, it was not until the late 1960s that levels of trade relative to GDP again attained the magnitudes they had reached at the turn of the century, and that the internationalization of capitalism seemed once again to be on the agenda. Since about 1970, the outward expansion of capitalism has turned into a flood, and the degree of interpenetration of the major capitalist economies has given rise to a situation that is more properly described as incipient globalization rather than internationalization, i.e. a situation in which national economies are evolving from a condition in which they are less like billiard balls in holistic interaction than they

[1] J. E. Thompson and S. D. Krasner, 'Global transactions and the consolidation of sovereignty', in E. O. Czempiel and J. N. Rosenau (eds.), *Global Changes and Theoretical Challenges*, Lexington: Lexington Books, 1989, pp. 195–219.

are permeable entities in various states of amalgamation with one another.

Hirst and Thompson have recently mounted a sharp critique of the writings of a group of scholars whom they label 'radical globalists', and who, they aver, have proclaimed that full globalization already exists as a more or less realized state of the world.[2] These scholars are taken to task by Hirst and Thompson on the grounds that the current situation is one that falls far short of the dissolution of distinctive national economies and the formation of a truly fluid global system, just as Krugman has also recently assailed many of the wilder claims made by a number of business commentators who ascribe every domestic ill to the effects of foreign economic competition.[3] These critiques no doubt sound a salutory note of warning about tendencies to over-exaggerate the extent to which globalization has actually moved forward over the last couple of decades, but they are, in the end, diversionary. Current empirical trends point unambiguously toward the deepening global ramification of capitalist production relations, not to mention the accelerating world-wide diffusion of social and cultural phenomena. There are also theoretical grounds, as I shall contend later, for taking seriously the prospect of eventual full globalization; and the fact that we are by all appearances in the early phases of the process should not divert us from the intellectual and political tasks of seeking to comprehend its long-term meaning. Hirst and Thompson make much of the fact that, over the greater part of the twentieth century, national economic openness as measured by foreign trade relative to GDP failed to reach the levels it had attained at the end of the nineteenth century. But another interpretation of the same datum is that the inter-war interlude was an aberration away from a trend toward world-wide economic integration that was already strongly in evidence a century ago, and that has now been decisively re-established.

This is not to say that major recrudescences of international political instability and uncertainty will not reverse the trend again in the future. The evidence suggests that we are now moving slowly but

---

[2] P. Hirst and G. Thompson, *Globalization in Question*, Cambridge: Polity Press, 1996.

[3] P. Krugman, *Pop Internationalism*, Cambridge, Mass.: MIT Press, 1996. See also R. Wade, 'Globalization and its limits: reports of the death of the national economy are greatly exaggerated', in S. Berger and R. Dore (eds.), *National Diversity and Global Capitalism*, Ithaca, NY: Cornell University Press, 1996, pp. 60–88.

steadily in the direction of a break-up of national capitalisms, in the sense that an ever-increasing openness and interdependence of economic systems is occurring at the global scale. However, and to repeat, we are still very far indeed from its hypothetical point of conclusion.

FROM INTERNATIONALIZATION TO GLOBALIZATION:
THE POST-WAR PERIOD

Some key historical markers

More than anything else, the initiatory event of the post-war trend to global economic openness and interdependence was the United Nations Monetary and Financial Conference held at Bretton Woods, New Hampshire, in July 1944. The Bretton Woods Conference, as it came to be known, sought to establish the basic ground-rules for a prospective post-war international economic order, and above all to work out the arrangements for an international currency system based on fixed exchange rates and the gold standard.[4] Two major financial institutions, the International Bank for Reconstruction and Development (IBRD) and the International Monetary Fund (IMF), were established under the aegis of the United Nations as an outcome of the conference, and both of them have continued to play important roles over the entire post-war period in helping to promote and integrate international development. The principal function of the IBRD, more familiarly known as the World Bank, is to make loans to member governments for specific development projects, while the IMF ensures international monetary cooperation and the stabilization of foreign exchange rates; in particular, the IMF helps member governments over periods of temporary difficulty as a result of balance of payments problems.

In 1947 the General Agreement on Tariffs and Trade (GATT) was established to regulate trade between the main capitalist countries. (Japan joined later, in 1955.) GATT has consistently pushed for the reduction of international trade barriers and has successfully secured significant rounds of tariff reductions and, in its new guise as the World Trade Organization, formed in 1994–5, it continues to be an aggressive

---

[4] R. Gilpin, *The Political Economy of International Relations*, Princeton: Princeton University Press, 1987.

force for free trade. Under the hegemonic leadership of the United States, these and a succession of analogous arrangements (including the Marshall Plan in the period 1948–51) became the foundations for rapid expansion of international commerce and exchange over the post-war years just as they served as bulwarks of the world anti-communist coalition that endured from the 1950s to the 1980s.

Under the aegis of this *Pax Americana*, the Western European and Japanese economies developed apace in the 1950s and 1960s and the foundations for a durable and growing international capitalist system were set in place. Even so, the very success of the system was in part responsible for a series of marked instabilities that began to make their appearance in the 1970s, undercutting US economic hegemony and setting the scene for a transition from internationalization as such to full-blown globalization.

The symbolic event marking the beginning of this transition was the decision by US President Richard Nixon in 1971 to remove the dollar from the gold standard. Within two years of this decision, the currencies of all the leading capitalist countries were floating, lead-ing to vastly augmented speculative waves of foreign exchange trans-actions around the world. The international oil shocks of the mid- and late 1970s exacerbated the climate of fiscal insecurity and dramatic-ally underlined the increasing reliance of national economies on one another. At the same time, the continued rise of Japan and the emer-gence of newly industrializing countries like Mexico, Brazil, and the tigers of East and South-east Asia caused major surges in world trade and capital flows, creating intensified competition for the fordist mass-production industries of North America and Western Europe, and in turn encouraging a massive shift of branch plants to overseas loca-tions in search of cheaper production sites.

In the new, more open, more competitive, and markedly less inter-ventionist political realities that were beginning to materialize in the wake of the relative decline of fordism and national keynesianism in the early 1980s, the globalization of the capitalist economic order continued its rapid, if erratic, forward advance. Many new and resur-gent production sectors were now injecting large volumes of output into world trade alongside more traditional items of international commerce, thus enlarging global commodity chains. And, with the demise of the Soviet Union and the ending of the Cold War at the end of the 1980s, the stage was now set for further massive expansion of the international system as the risk of serious and uncontrollable political and military disruptions on the international scene seemed to diminish.

International trade and economic openness

One of the most direct and dramatic indices of the increasing economic integration marking the post-war world is foreign trade. In 1960 total world merchandise exports represented just 5.8% of world GDP and merchandise imports represented 6.1%; by 1993 these figures were 15.8% and 15.4% respectively,[5] representing an increase that is all the more significant in that it is defined purely in relation to GDP, which itself grew rapidly over the same period. Total world merchandise exports and imports in 1993 totalled $3.6 and $3.7 trillion, respectively. In absolute terms, these figures represent close to a sixfold real growth in world merchandise trade between 1960 and the early 1990s. International trade in services has expanded even more rapidly than merchandise trade, and today aggregate world exports (or imports) of services add about a further $1 trillion to the merchandise trade data.

Figure 3.1 maps out trends in GDP and international trade (merchandise plus services) for OECD countries indexed to the base year 1960, and both the absolute and relative pace of trade expansion is brought clearly to the fore. The OECD, which basically consists of the Triad countries of North America, Western Europe, and Japan, accounts for some 70% of all world trade. Figure 3.2 shows the recent and ever-increasing importance of services in US exports and imports, and in passing underlines the marked acceleration of US trade in general since about 1970.

While the interpenetration of national economies has in general been increasing greatly over the last few decades, as is suggested by the trade data discussed above, its degree of intensity varies widely from case to case. Of the many factors underlying this variability, one of the most significant is related simply to overall country size. As Figure 3.3 indicates, countries with relatively small GDPs tend to be much more open to trade than those with large GDPs. For example, Luxembourg, with a GDP of $14.0 billion in 1994, had exports that were equal to 92.2% of GDP and imports equal to 84.1%; the USA had a GDP of $6,649.8 billion in the same year but its exports were only 10.6% of this amount and its imports 12.3%.

---

[5] UN, *Statistical Yearbook*, New York: United Nations (annual).

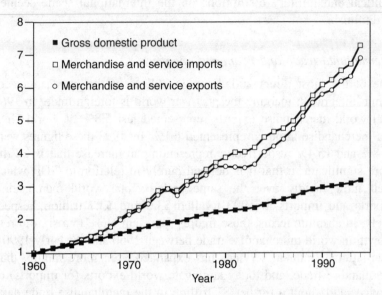

FIG. 3.1. GDP and merchandise/service exports and imports for OECD
countries 1960–1994 (1960 = 1)

Original data in constant dollars.

Source of data: OECD, *National Accounts*, Paris: Organisation for Economic Cooperation
and Development (annual).

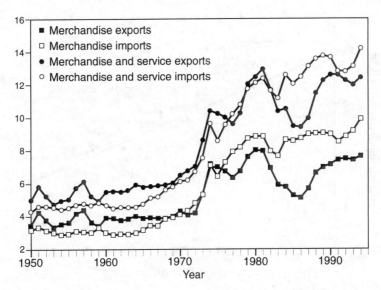

FIG. 3.2. US exports and imports as a percentage of gross domestic product, 1950–1994

Source of data: US Department of Commerce, Bureau of the Census, *Statistical Abstract of the United States*, Washington (annual).

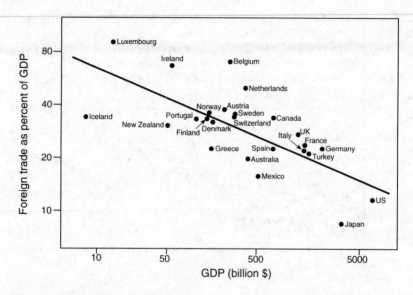

FIG. 3.3. Foreign trade as a percentage of gross domestic product in relation to gross domestic product for OECD countries, 1994

Foreign trade is measured as $\frac{1}{2}$(exports + imports).

The equation of the regression line is $y = 105.7x^{-0.217}$, with $R^2 = 0.49$.

Source of data: OECD, *National Accounts*, Paris: Organisation for Economic Cooperation and Development (annual).

This statistically significant relationship between openness and size of national economies can be accounted for largely in terms of scale effects and the division of labor. Hence large economic systems can maintain high levels of development and diversity of consumption on the basis of economies of scale in production and extended social divisions of labor within the confines of their own borders, whereas small economic systems can achieve the same effects only by accepting a more thorough-going integration into the international division of labor.[6] An evident corollary is that sub-national regional economic complexes, which are by definition small and specialized relative to the national contexts in which they find themselves, are likely to be especially open and interdependent, at least in the more advanced economies. A further corollary is that, in a prospective world of regions, export orientation is apt to be the high road to economic prosperity (though it may be counterbalanced by social and cultural costs), and doubly so—as the new trade theory predicts—because there are almost always potent increasing returns effects to be secured at the point of production.[7] No doubt we might expect to find that variations in average GDP per capita will also have a significant effect on the economic openness of countries and regions. In other words, all else being equal, we can anticipate that national and regional economies will trade proportionally more as GDP per capita increases, both because prosperity is in part dependent on success in export activities, and because higher incomes lead to a greater demand for imports.

The complex interrelations between openness to trade, size of national economy, and GDP per capita for OECD countries over the period 1960–94 are summarized in Table 3.1, which shows the results of a series of cross-section regression analyses at five-year intervals. The dependent variable in these regressions is defined as the ratio of external trade to GDP (representing openness), while the independent variables are total GDP and GDP per capita, with all monetary values converted into constant 1990 dollars. Three main propensities can be discerned in the results presented. First, as indicated by the rising values of the constant term over time, there is a definite tendency for economic openness to increase as a historical trend. Second, openness

[6] P. J. Katzenstein, *Small States in World Markets: Industrial Policy in Europe*, Ithaca, NY: Cornell University Press, 1985.

[7] P. Krugman, *Geography and Trade*, Leuven: Leuven University Press, 1991.

TABLE 3.1. Regression analysis of the relations between trade, total GDP, and GDP per capita, OECD countries, 1960–1994

	Constant	GDP in $bn (log)		GDP per capita (log)		R^2	Standard deviation of GDP per capita values across countries
		Coefficient	*t*-value	Coefficient	*t*-value		
1960	4.16	−0.3508	7.43	0.4849	8.69	0.77	5875.6
1965	4.19	−0.3293	7.68	0.4452	8.76	0.78	7870.8
1970	4.28	−0.3116	7.46	0.4409	8.61	0.77	9289.6
1975	4.12	−0.2637	7.14	0.4052	8.81	0.78	10376.9
1980	4.14	−0.2279	5.92	0.3729	7.33	0.72	9051.8
1985	5.08	−0.2340	5.09	0.3334	4.81	0.60	8852.8
1990	5.66	−0.2235	4.52	0.2900	2.39	0.53	8790.9
1994	6.89	−0.2274	4.85	0.2738	1.57	0.54	7268.2

Notes: The dependent variable is represented by $\frac{1}{2}$(exports + imports) as a percentage of GDP. Original data defined in terms of constant 1990 dollars; $N = 25$.

Source: of data: OECD, *National Accounts*, Paris: Organisation for Economic Cooperation and Development (annual).

displays a consistently inverse and statistically significant relationship to total GDP, though the relationship has a tendency to weaken over time. Third, the effect of GDP per capita on openness is positive and extremely significant in the 1960s and 1970s, but then becomes much less influential in the 1980s and 1990s, and is quite insignificant in 1994.

The results set out in Table 3.1 thus confirm our expectations, though all the statistical relationships identified tend to diminish in strength as we move from the 1960s to the 1990s. This circumstance, troubling perhaps at first glance, turns out to be entirely consistent with the overall thrust of the analysis. In fact, the raw data reveal that there is no shift whatever to diminished economic openness among OECD countries. What we are observing in the complex quantitative information set forth in Table 3.1 is rather the continued expansion of external trade over the 1960s, 1970s, 1980s, and 1990s, but in a situation where:

1. the smaller advanced economies are today so thoroughly open that continued expansion of trade *relative* to GDP is no longer feasible on a large scale, whereas larger economies are now opening up to external trade at a much more rapid pace than formerly; and
2. a marked convergence of levels of GDP per capita has been occurring among OECD countries since 1975 (as revealed by the last column of Table 3.1), so that differentials in the effect of this variable on trade have been progressively muted.

These remarks are given added force if we look at similar data for a much wider set of (developed and underdeveloped) economies. Using the same variables as those designated in Table 3.1, a logarithmic regression analysis of trade levels relative to GDP for all 111 UN member countries for which data were available in 1992 yields an overall R^2 equal to a modest but extremely significant 0.22.[8] In line with expectations, the regression coefficient for aggregate GDP is negative and for GDP per capita it is positive. In the former case the value of the regression coefficient is -0.1631 (with $t = 5.46$); in the latter it is 0.1506 ($t = 3.54$). Thus, once we enlarge the empirical range of the GDP per capita variable so as to capture much higher

---

[8] Data for this exercise were taken from UN, *Statistical Yearbook.*

levels of variance, its role in explaining international trade patterns comes once more significantly into evidence.

Beyond trade

As important as trade may be as a cornerstone of and a symptom of diminishing levels of national economic autarchy, it is by no means the only or even the most important way in which this process has been occurring.

A major complementary factor in the drive to globalization is foreign direct investment (FDI), originating for the most part in the more economically advanced countries and proliferating throughout the world. This has resulted in the world-wide diffusion of branch plants owned by multinational corporations, with the consequence that these corporations have now moved into a dominating position as the coordinating agencies of modern global production systems. As much as one-third of all the foreign trade dealings of the United States now actually take the form of intra-firm trade, where the latter term signifies that exports and imports of goods and services are occurring between different affiliates of the same company.[9] The importance of multinational corporations in the world economy is indicated by the fact that the Fortune Global 500 companies earned a total revenue of $10,245 billion in 1994, representing an enormous 44.3% of world GDP. By the mid-1990s, there were 38,541 parent companies in the world and 251,450 dependent foreign affiliates. As much as 89.1% of the former were located in developed countries, particularly France, Germany, Japan, the United Kingdom and the USA, while 62.9% of the latter were located in lesser developed countries. The world's ten largest multinational corporations are listed in Table 3.2, which also provides data indicating that in all cases significant proportions of their assets and operating activities are located outside of the home country. By 1991 the total sales of all foreign subsidiaries of multinationals exceeded world exports by a substantial margin,[10] with US foreign affiliate sales exceeding US exports by a factor of four, and Japanese foreign affiliate sales exceeding Japanese exports by a factor

[9] OECD, *Intrafirm Trade*, Paris: Organisation for Economic Cooperation and Development, 1993.

[10] R. Vernon, 'Passing through regionalism: the transition to global markets', *The World Economy*, 19 (1996): 621–33.

TABLE 3.2. The top ten multinational corporations ranked by foreign assets, 1994

Corporation	Country	Industry	Assets ($bn)		Sales ($bn)		Employment ('000)	
			Total	Foreign	Total	Foreign	Total	Foreign
Royal Dutch Shell	UK/ Netherlands	Petroleum	102.0	63.7	94.8	51.1	106	79
Ford	USA	Motor vehicles & parts	219.4	60.6	128.4	38.1	338	97
Exxon	USA	Petroleum	87.9	56.2	113.9	72.3	86	55
General Motors	USA	Motor vehicles & parts	198.6	n.a.	152.2	44.0	693	178
IBM	USA	Computers	81.1	43.9	64.1	39.9	220	116
Volkswagen	Germany	Motor vehicles & parts	52.4	n.a.	49.3	29.0	242	97
General Electric	USA	Electronics	251.5	33.9	59.3	11.9	216	36
Toyota	Japan	Motor vehicles & parts	116.8	n.a.	91.3	37.2	173	28
Daimler– Benz	Germany	Transport & communications	66.5	27.9	74.0	46.3	331	79
Elf Acquitaine	France	Petroleum	48.9	n.a.	38.9	26.2	90	44

Source: UNCTAD, *World Investment Report, 1996: Investment, Trade and International Policy Arrangements: Overview*, New York and Geneva: United Nations, 1996.

of two. The aggregate capital value of all foreign affiliates at all locations in the world was assessed at $2.4 trillion in 1994, and in the same year total new FDI capital investments were $222 billion, which is close to about 1% of world GDP.[11]

Table 3.3 provides data on stocks and flows of foreign direct investments for OECD countries over the period 1981–94. Even after discounting for the effects of inflation, the rate of growth of these investments over the last two decades has been extraordinarily high, with total stocks held by OECD countries increasing more than threefold in real terms over the fourteen-year period identified in the table. Outflows and inflows of foreign direct investments have a tendency to vary greatly from year to year, above all in response to changes in the business cycle, but the general trend is unambiguously positive. In recent years, too, their expansion has far outstripped even the growth of foreign trade, as more and more private firms seek out the advantages of overseas locations for affiliate operations. Moreover, and the point is important for future reference, the advantages of such locations are to an increasing extent being assessed by multinational corporations not just in terms of their broad national context, but also in terms of their very specific regional attributes.

Additionally, international monetary transactions have been spiralling uncontrollably upward in recent years. Enormous amounts of liquid capital now move from country to country in a fraction of a second in response to subtle shifts in economic trends in different countries. Average global foreign exchange transactions are currently estimated to be in the range of $1 trillion *daily*, and in 1993 the foreign assets of deposit banks world-wide amounted to $7 trillion,[12] a figure that represents just under one-third of world GDP. The sheer magnitude of the liquid assets now circulating the globe on a daily basis in search of short-term profits is itself sufficient to circumscribe the decision-making powers of individual governments, and in times of international financial crisis it can, and does, imperil the policies of central banks.

All of this economic effervescence in the international sphere has been facilitated by continual lowering of tariff barriers and other institutional impediments to trade, as well as by dramatic improvements

---

[11] UNCTAD, *World Investment Report*, New York and Geneva: United Nations, 1995.
[12] IMF, *International Statistics Financial Yearbook*, Washington: International Monetary Fund, 1993.

TABLE 3.3. Direct investment position abroad together with annual outflows and inflows of foreign direct investments, OECD countries, 1981–1994

	Billions of current dollars			Billions of constant 1994 dollars		
	Direct investment position abroad	Outflows	Inflows	Direct investment position abroad	Outflows	Inflows
1981	474.6	48.5	41.0	672.8	68.8	58.1
1982	472.8	25.6	30.4	634.0	34.3	40.8
1983	486.6	33.1	33.7	634.8	43.2	44.0
1984	512.1	45.1	41.4	652.8	57.5	52.8
1985	561.2	56.4	41.7	700.1	70.4	52.0
1986	690.3	85.4	67.2	843.8	104.4	82.1
1987	884.7	129.9	115.4	1062.1	155.9	138.5
1988	1013.4	159.1	132.1	1188.9	186.7	155.0
1989	1251.6	205.9	168.2	1422.4	234.0	191.1
1990	1509.1	216.3	164.4	1646.6	236.0	179.4
1991	1663.9	178.9	117.2	1761.1	189.3	124.0
1992	1734.5	163.8	100.5	1801.7	170.1	104.4
1993	1883.4	166.6	105.4	1922.1	170.0	107.6
1994	2124.0	187.0	142.1	2124.0	187.0	142.1

Source: OECD, *International Direct Investment Statistics Yearbook*, Paris: Organisation for Economic Cooperation and Development (annual).

in transportation and communication technologies. Among the many important developments in this domain may be mentioned the advent of large-scale container transport by land and sea, the proliferation of inexpensive international air connections, and the development of world-wide electronic communications systems of all sorts, including the Internet. As a consequence, the costs of transacting between different countries are progressively falling, while the velocity of circulation of people, goods, services, and information has been increasing exponentially. Hence, virtually every index of international interaction, from trade flows to tourism and from airline passengers to telephone calls, is currently at a historical peak, and commodities like Coca-Cola, McDonald's hamburgers, Nike athletic shoes, the Sony Walkman, or Benetton's casual fashions have near-universal market penetration. An evident dilemma resulting from this state of affairs is the cultural clashes that occur as different societies across the globe come more and more intimately into contact with one another.

It might be said, indeed, that as we approach the dawn of the twenty-first century individual national capitalisms are actually beginning to merge together (though they are far from having yet merged) into a much more integrated system of socio-economic relations. To an ever-increasing extent, national governments are finding that their capacity to intermediate between their internal realms and extra-national economic events is in jeopardy. Even in the United States, with its low (but rapidly growing) rate of foreign trade relative to GDP, the impacts of accelerating globalization on finance, production, and employment are enormous. In particular, the impacts on selective sectors and regions are often quite critical, as illustrated by such hapless cases as Detroit and Pittsburgh in the 1970s, or the success stories of Silicon Valley and Hollywood today—although, as Lawrence has recently pointed out in a careful empirical study, the effects of foreign trade on the average wages of low-income workers in the United States have generally been exaggerated.[13] If the United States is still relatively sheltered from the vagaries of world markets, this can be expected to change as the country becomes more deeply embroiled in a global system of economic relationships. When we consider small or medium-sized countries such as Singapore, Taiwan, New Zealand,

---

[13] R. Z. Lawrence, *Single World, Divided Nations? International Trade and OECD Labor Markets*, Paris: OECD Development Centre, 1996.

Switzerland, or Mexico, the internal consequences of externalization are liable to be very marked indeed.

Questions of governance

The broad effect of the trends described above is a relentless erosion of the borders between individual national economies and a shift in the pattern of world development from a network of interacting national economies toward a single globally integrating economic system.

Concomitantly, different governance measures are constantly being put into place to deal with the mounting problems generated by this situation. These measures have mushroomed in piecemeal fashion, largely as a system of stopgap measures, and the one international institution that has mimicked the form of a centralized parliamentary governmental structure—the United Nations—has not, up to now, been notably successful in practical terms. Instead, issues of governance at the global level are typically dealt with through the development of a complex and largely uncoordinated structure of international regimes in the form of conventions and tacit agreements or special-purpose regulatory bodies and intergovernmental commissions.[14]

These different sorts of institution have been multiplying markedly of late. Among the more prominent of them are the G7 meetings, the World Bank, the FAO, ILO, IMF, OECD, UNCTAD, and the WTO, though this only a small set of examples out of a vast field of similar phenomena. According to one information source, as many as 5,401 international intergovernmental associations were identifiable in 1994, and, even more remarkable, 31,085 non-governmental international associations were in evidence, a twenty-five-fold growth overall since 1960.[15] These non-governmental associations cover an exceptionally wide gamut of interests and activities, including international health, civil rights, welfare, women's issues, the environment, scientific research, economic development, and so on; and, despite

[14] J. A. Camilleri and J. Falk, *The End of Sovereignty? The Politics of a Shrinking and Fragmenting World*, Aldershot: Edward Elgar, 1992; D. Deudney, 'Binding sovereigns: authorities, structures, and geopolitics in Philadelphian systems', in T. J. Biersteker and C. Weber (eds.), *State Sovereignty as Social Construct*, Cambridge: Cambridge University Press, 1996, pp. 190–239; R. O. Keohane, *International Institutions and State Power: Essays in International Relations Theory*, Boulder, Colo.: Westview Press, 1989.

[15] Union of International Associations, *Yearbook of International Associations*, Munich: K. G. Saur, 1995.

their purely civil status, they often play important roles in governance issues of global scope.[16]

The palpable erosion of the boundaries between sovereign states over the post-war decades has also been accompanied and hastened by the formation of a number of plurinational economic and political alliances, as mentioned in Chapter 2. Notwithstanding the mixed record of these alliances, they are a further expression of the trend toward political reorganization at supra-state levels, for they are institutional arrangements within which individual countries essentially give up elements of their national sovereignty in exchange for wider access to markets and resources in a context of strong legislatively based guarantees of cooperation. With the scheduled monetary merger of at least a core group of countries in the European Union on 1 January 1999, the process will have been carried to a historically new peak of development.

In the long run, these alliances may turn out to be either stable elements of the emerging world system, or simply way-stations on the long road to full globalization. The ultimate end-point of this evolutionary process remains, of course, entirely beyond our apprehension at this stage in history. Will the eventual global order of capitalism consist primarily of a loose federation of plurinational alliances? a world economic directorate? a dense regime of criss-crossing contractual obligations? The general direction of change, however, is unambiguous. At a minimum, it most assuredly entails the continued loss of national economic autonomy so that the sovereign political identity of the assets, outputs, and institutions of the economy becomes increasingly difficult to ascertain, and the social relations of production become ever more tightly linked together in world-wide structures of interdependence.[17]

THE GEOGRAPHY OF GLOBALIZATION

The trends delineated in the previous section are inscribed in a changing pattern of intra-national and international spatial relationships that

---

[16] L. Gordenker and T. G. Weiss, 'Pluralizing global governance: analytical approaches and dimensions', in T. G. Weiss and L. Gordenker (eds.), *NGOs, the UN, and Global Governance*, Boulder, Colo.: Lynne Rienner, 1996, pp. 17–47.

[17] Rosecrance, 'The rise of the virtual state', *Foreign Affairs*, 75 (1996): 45–61.

has been observable in its essentials virtually from the origins of capitalism. Here I am referring to the persistent division of geographic space into core areas and peripheral areas, as mentioned in Chapter 2. Since at least the 1950s, there have been several notable efforts to explain these sorts of division—and their expression in the geography of development and trade—in terms of various conceptions of cumulative causation or hysteresis. Most of these efforts are also characterized by aspirations to go beyond the static Ricardian notion of comparative advantage as a fixed condition defined by pre-given natural endowments.

Although Wallerstein is the master theorist and historian of the core–periphery model at the world scale (as well as the originator of the notion of the semi-periphery), the roots of the idea go back to the writings of Myrdal and Hirschman in the late 1950s.[18] These theorists were concerned at the outset to explain why within-country regional differences in levels of income and development were typically so pronounced in North America and Western Europe. In order to deal with this problem, they invoked two main sets of notions:

1. 'backwash' or 'polarization' (the former is Myrdal's term, the latter Hirschman's), by which they meant a tendency for major industrial regions to grow by means of their own magnet-like ability to draw in people and resources from distant locations; and
2. 'spread' or 'trickle-down', signifying the countervailing flow of growth effects from more developed to less developed regions via increased spending in core regions on the products of the periphery, and governmental efforts to raise incomes and opportunity levels in the periphery.

These ideas stimulated intense debate over the 1960s about the relative intensity of backwash (polarization) and spread (trickle-down) effects and their differential impacts on growth rates in core and peripheral areas. For our purposes, however, their pertinence is that they were subsequently picked up and reworked in various ways by theorists of the new international order.

Thus, in the 1970s Amin and Frank linked the core–periphery model with theories of colonial and neo-colonial exploitation at the

---

[18] G. Myrdal, *Rich Lands and Poor*, New York: Harper and Row, 1957; A. Hirschman, *The Strategy of Economic Development*, New Haven: Yale University Press, 1958.

world scale.[19] They argued that spatially uneven and unequal forms of development were not only endemic to capitalism but also destined to become more sharply apparent with the passage of time, so that the gap between the advanced economies and the Third World would only tend to widen. In a book published in 1972, Emmanuel argued specifically that the mechanism underlying exacerbated unequal development in the world system could be found in the logic of international trade, and that Third World countries were essentially subsidizing the First World whenever the low-wage, labor-intensive products of the former were exchanged for the high-wage, capital-intensive products of the latter.[20]

A further cycle of investigations of world capitalism based on the core–periphery model was set in motion by a group of German researchers at the end of the 1970s who suggested that a so-called new international division of labor was making its appearance, with the more economically advanced countries becoming specialized in production based on high-wage white-collar labor while the less advanced countries were turning into repositories of blue-collar labor.[21] The agents of this transformation were said to be the burgeoning multinational corporations, which were to an increasing degree locating their high-end administrative, research, and production activities in the skilled-labor economies of North America, Western Europe, and Japan, while allocating their routine assembly functions to low-wage countries of the Third World, most especially Asia and Latin America. This locational pattern was above all observable in the case of large fordist-style multinationals employing huge numbers of assembly workers in routine, low-grade jobs, with branch plants being pushed out into the world periphery by the cost competition that was intensifying greatly as globalization worked its course.

We need not linger here over the theoretical and substantive niceties of these approaches. Each of them captures something of the macro-

---

[19] S. Amin, *Le Développement Inegal*, Paris: Les Editions de Minuit, 1973; A. G. Frank, *Dependent Accumulation and Underdevelopment*, New York: Monthly Review Press, 1979.

[20] A. Emmanuel, *Unequal Exchange: A Study of the Imperialism of Trade*, New York: Monthly Review Press, 1972.

[21] F. Fröbel, J. Heinrichs, and O. Kreye, *The New International Division of Labour*, Cambridge: Cambridge University Press, 1980. An extended discussion and critique of the new international division of labor thesis can be found in J. Henderson, *The Globalisation of High-Technology Production: Society, Space and Semiconductors in the Restructuring of the Modern World*, London: Routledge, 1989.

geographic logic and dynamics of the modern world. In different ways, Ricardian comparative advantage, the Myrdal–Hirschman approach, uneven development and exchange, and the new international division of labor theory (not to forget the Wallersteinian synthesis) describe processes and phenomena that continue to leave their mark on world-wide spatial patterns of development and trade. Like all ideas, however, they are very much rooted in particular conjunctures of events and in on-going frameworks of political debate, and they can be questioned on many different grounds in the light of subsequent developments. They continue to suggest a number of fruitful lines of inquiry; however, in view of the rapid changes now going on at all geographic scales, as intimated in this and the previous chapter, some sort of re-synthesis would seem to be in order.

This prospective re-synthesis, it seems to me, needs to build upon and carry forward the key insights about a world system of centers, margins, and intermediate areas described above, but it also needs to be much more explicit about what Badie has called the 'new grammar of space' that is emerging at the end of the twentieth century.[22] Two intertwined moments of analysis must be taken very seriously in this enterprise. One of these, as we have seen, involves a thorough-going problematic of the global with its point of departure situated in the observation that the historical phenomenon of the national economy has been a political more than a strictly economic arrangement, and that this arrangement is now in course of being severely eroded by the robust outward drive of capitalism. The other is the concomitant need for a coherent account of the emergence of a world-wide system of regional economies constituting the main spatial nuclei of the new global economy.[23] The linkage between the two (to be more fully investigated in Chapter 5) is constituted in part by what we might term a neo-Listian theory of regional development, in which the socially and politically constructed competitive advantages of particular places become the shifting foundations of the composite economic geography of the world system.

[22] B. Badie, *La Fin des Territoires*, Paris: Fayard, 1995.
[23] See e.g. J. Agnew and S. Corbridge, *Mastering Space: Hegemony, Territory, and International Political Economy*, London: Routledge, 1995; A. Amin and N. Thrift, 'Neo-Marshallian nodes in global networks', *International Journal of Urban and Regional Research*, 16 (1992): 571–87; A. J. Scott, 'Regional motors of the global economy', *Futures*, 28: 391–411; M. Storper, 'The limits to globalization: technology districts and international trade', *Economic Geography*, 68: 60–93.

In parallel with this changing grammar of space, a diffusion of gov-ernance functions away from the classical sovereign state seems to be in progress. That said, an important reservation remains. Despite this spreading out of functions, the sovereign state continues to play a major role in the modern world, and any claims about its imminent demise must be viewed with caution. Those, like Ohmae, who fore-see its virtual dissolution fail, in particular, to take into account the social and above all perhaps the cultural pressures—as opposed to the economic relations—that continue to make the state and the nation potent political realities in the contemporary world.[24]

---

[24] K. Ohmae, *The End of the Nation State*, New York: Free Press, 1995.

4

The Global Mosaic of Regional Economies

Although the economic interconnections between different locations across the globe are expanding at a rapid pace, the state of the world remains far indeed from anything even approaching spatial liquefaction. Localized processes of growth and development have actually been accentuated by globalization, and this is nowhere more apparent than in the case of those dense concentrations of capital and human labor now multiplying throughout the world in the guise of large metropolitan areas. The latter constitute the elemental choremes, as it were, of the ascending world economic system, and as such they function as the basic units of a new global mosaic of regional economies.

Dynamic urban regions, of course, have been persistent elements of the landscape of capitalism over both the nineteenth and twentieth centuries. Today, however, their importance assumes added weight by reason of the combined effects of (*a*) the secular lowering of the economic and political boundaries between different places, resulting in the progressive incorporation of urban regions into vastly extended networks of linkages, and (*b*) the developmental take-off of many formerly marginal areas, leading to the world-wide extension of large-scale urbanization.

Three main remarks must be made here. First, and to reiterate, major metropolitan areas continue to expand at a remarkable rate—contrary to a commonly held view that new transportation and communication technologies are beginning to subvert urbanization processes. Second, the world's metropolitan areas are increasingly enmeshed in expansive spatial divisions of labor as expressed in part in inter-regional commodity chains stretching across the globe.[1] Third, precisely because of the lowering of economic and political boundaries, these events are to lesser and lesser degrees controllable by the sovereign state, which, by the same token, finds it increasingly difficult to protect individual regions and sectors within its purview from the shocks and

---

[1] G. Gereffi and M. Korzeniewicz (eds.), *Commodity Chains and Global Capitalism*, Westport, Conn.: Greenwood Press, 1994.

pressures that they inevitably feel on occasions as globalization intensifies. In response to this latter state of affairs, many regions in many different parts of the world are starting to cast about for new ways to assert their own economic interests, to build localized competitive advantages serving their specific needs, and to assert their political individuality and identity.

CONTOURS OF THE GLOBAL MOSAIC

The global mosaic of regional economies alluded to above comprises a series of densely developed geographic spaces scattered across the globe, each constituted by (*a*) a central nucleus (e.g. a metropolitan area or a group of coterminous metropolitan areas), and (*b*) a surrounding dependent hinterland of variable radius. This set of spaces is superimposed upon and intersects with swaths of much less well developed territory toward the extensive margins of capitalist development. Any attempt to understand the contours of this entire system must in part, at least, come to terms with the ubiquitous phenomenon of demographic and economic clustering in geographic space.

The clustering of population

Throughout the post-war decades, the main nodes of the mosaic have grown rapidly in terms of population, and additional nodes have continually sprung up at new locations all over the world. Today, urban areas of all sizes account for as much as 44.8% of the world's population, with more developed countries being characterized by an average urbanization quotient of 74.7% and less developed countries by a quotient of 37.0%.[2]

On the more narrowly defined basis of metropolitan areas with populations of 1 million or more—of which there was a total of 272 in 1990—the percentage of the world's population accounted for is 14.0%, though this rises to 25.6% on average in the more economically advanced countries. At the turn of the century, the phenomenon of the 'million city' was considered to be an unusual if not an aberrant occurrence, limited for the most part to the special case of capital cities. At the present time, it is a common feature of daily experience in

---

[2] UN, *World Urbanization Prospects*, New York: United Nations, 1995.

many different areas of the world (see Figure 4.1); and, as shown by the data laid out in Table 4.1, the number of metropolitan areas with a population of at least 1 million more than tripled between 1950 and 1990.

Table 4.2 provides data on the fifteen largest metropolitan areas in the world at different points in time. In 1950 these areas accounted for a total population of 82.5 million; by 1970 their aggregate population had grown to 140.2 million, and by 1990 to 189.6 million. Paradoxically, these very largest metropolitan areas are becoming more concentrated in poorer countries and less so in richer countries—in 1950 as many as two-thirds of them were located in the developed capitalist world, but by 1990 this fraction had fallen to just one-third. Most of the recent population growth of these and other large metropolitan areas is not so much the result of natural increase as it is an outcome of complex systems of migration from regions of lower economic opportunity to regions of higher economic opportunity, e.g. from rural to urban areas, and from lesser developed countries to more economically advanced countries. In poorer parts of the world, vigorous inward migration to cities often results in what is occasionally described as macrocephalic urban growth (i.e. pathological over-development of the largest city), which in turn is an echo of the relative scarcity of economic opportunities across space, with the concomitant piling up of migrants at only a few locations as the invariable result. The persistence of these migration streams into metropolitan areas throughout the world is nonetheless testimony to the continuing economic vitality of the urban process in contemporary capitalism.

The clustering of economic activities

The motive force behind this long-run trend to expansion and multiplication of large urban regions is lodged above all in the general thrust of economic growth and its peculiar spatial resolution as an uneven pattern of development focused on a relatively small number of giant agglomerations.

As a first approximation, we can think of the economies of large urban regions as being separable into basic and non-basic production activities.[3] The former consist of enterprises that export their outputs

---

[3] J. W. Alexander, 'The basic-nonbasic concept of urban economic functions', *Economic Geography*, 30 (1954): 246–61; R. B. Andrews, 'The mechanics of the urban economic base', *Land Economics*, 29 (1953): 321–33.

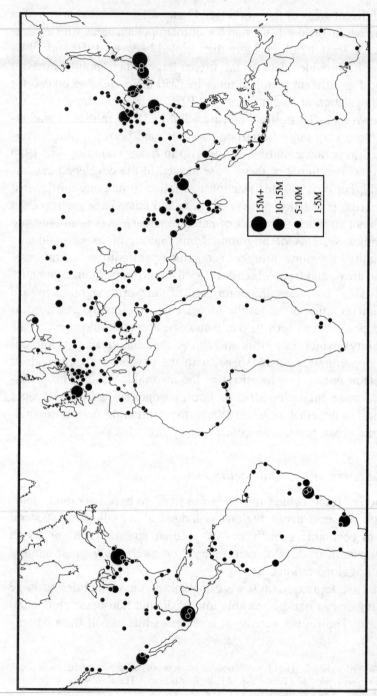

FIG. 4.1. Current world distribution of metropolitan areas with populations greater than 1 million.
Source of data: UN, *World Urbanization Prospects.* New York: United Nations, 1995.

TABLE 4.1. The number of large metropolitan areas in the world, 1950, 1970, and 1990

Population category (millions)	Number of metropolitan areas		
	1950	1970	1990
1–5	75	144	249
5–10	7	18	21
10+	1	3	12
Total	83	165	272

Source: UN, *World Urbanization Prospects*, New York: United Nations, 1995.

Global Mosaic of Regional Economies

TABLE 4.2. The fifteen largest metropolitan areas in the world, 1950, 1970, and 1990

Population (millions)

1950		1970		1990	
New York	12.3	Tokyo	16.5	Tokyo	25.0
London	8.7	New York	16.2	New York	16.1
Tokyo	6.9	Shanghai	11.2	Mexico	15.1
Paris	5.4	Osaka	9.4	São Paulo	14.8
Moscow	5.4	Mexico	9.1	Shanghai	13.5
Shanghai	5.3	London	8.6	Bombay	12.2
Essen	5.3	Paris	8.5	Los Angeles	11.5
Buenos Aires	5.0	Buenos Aires	8.4	Beijing	10.9
Chicago	4.9	Los Angeles	8.4	Calcutta	10.7
Calcutta	4.4	Beijing	8.1	Buenos Aires	10.6
Osaka	4.1	São Paulo	8.1	Seoul	10.6
Los Angeles	4.0	Moscow	7.1	Osaka	10.5
Beijing	3.9	Rio de Janeiro	7.0	Rio de Janeiro	9.5
Milan	3.6	Calcutta	6.9	Paris	9.3
Berlin	3.3	Chicago	6.7	Tianjin	9.3
Total	82.5		140.2		189.6

Source: UN, *World Urbanization Prospects*, New York: United Nations, 1995.

beyond the boundaries of the urban area, and thus are the principal foundation of local prosperity. The latter produce goods and services for purely intra-regional consumption; despite their economic dependence on the base, they typically account for anywhere from 50% to 60% of total employment in any given region.[4] More sophisticated accounts of the urban economy unpack this simple twofold schema into any number of individual sectors, each of which in varying proportion sells its products in both local and extra-local markets. From this perspective, the local economy can then be described in a preliminary way as a system of production-*cum*-transactional operations, involving:

1. a regional nexus of input–output relations with firms buying and selling capital goods from one another in more or less expanded production sequences;
2. a purely sumptuary segment, serving the needs of the local populace and based in part on local inputs;
3. a structure of trade with other regions, such that surpluses of both capital goods and consumer goods are exported while deficits are made up by imports.

At the heart of any regional economy like this, we are liable to find an enormous diversity of manufacturing firms, service enterprises, and —to an ever-increasing degree in modern post-fordist cities—cultural-products providers. The latter are engaged in sectors such as fashion clothing, jewelry, publishing, films, television, multimedia, music, and so on. Official statistical classifications typically assign cultural-products sectors to disjoint manufacturing and service categories; but, given their massive importance in many large cities today, the distinctiveness of their final outputs, and their often global reach, it is useful to think of them as all belonging to the same broad classificatory unit,[5] and I shall refer to them in this way in subsequent chapters.

All of these production activities occur in dense urban concentrations, though we can almost always also find a complementary pattern of locational dispersal, which may even become dominant in some sectors at certain conjunctures depending on the interplay of technologies, labor

---

[4] J. V. Henderson, *Urban Development: Theory, Fact and Illusion*, New York: Oxford University Press, 1988.

[5] A. J. Scott, 'The craft, fashion, and cultural-products industries of Los Angeles: competitive dynamics and policy dilemmas in a multisectoral image-producing complex', *Annals of the Association of American Geographers*, 86 (1996): 306–23.

costs, market conditions, and so on. Moreover, individual concentrations have a propensity to display palpable forms of economic specialization, a feature that may be expected to intensify as they are further integrated into a global division of labor.

The spatial concentration of production has in fact been a chronic long-run feature of capitalist development, and it continues even today to be one of the major processes shaping and reshaping the economic geography of the world. For example, in the United States in 1992, as much as 51.3% of all manufacturing employment and 52.8% of all manufacturing value added was concentrated in metropolitan areas with a population of 1 million or more (see Table 4.3), of which there were just forty in 1990. In the two decades between 1972 and 1992, manufacturing employment in these forty metropolitan areas grew by 4.3% whereas in the country as a whole it declined by 3.9%; at the same time, manufacturing value added grew by 30.6% in the forty metropolitan areas, in contrast to a growth rate of 20.3% for the entire country. In addition, although Table 4.3 reveals that the three largest metropolitan areas in the United States (New York, Los Angeles, and Chicago) showed a significant decline in manufacturing employment between 1972 and 1992, they actually continue to be absolutely dominant centers of manufacturing activity in terms of both employment and value added (with the latter variable actually increasing in constant-dollar terms between 1972 and 1992). Significantly, manufacturing employment and value added expanded at extremely rapid rates from 1972 to 1992 in the remaining thirty-seven of the forty metropolitan areas. For comparative purposes, data on Japan for 1993 reveal that a little over one-third of the country's total 10.9 million employees in manufacturing were concentrated in just five prefectures, i.e. Aichi, Kanagawa, Osaka, Saitama, and Tokyo.[6]

In view of the absolute and relative shifts in the US economy from manufacturing to services, we might well have expected the manufacturing performance of large cities to have lagged more severely than it has done. By the same token, the service industry performance of large American cities has been remarkable in recent decades. This comment is underlined by the data presented in Table 4.4, showing that service industry receipts in the forty largest US metropolitan areas grew by as much as 174.0% between 1972 and 1992, whereas the

---

[6] *Japan Statistical Yearbook*, Tokyo: Statistics Bureau, Management and Coordination Agency, 1996.

TABLE 4.3. Manufacturing employment and value added in the forty US metropolitan areas with a population of 1 million or more in 1992

Population category (millions)	No. of metropolitan areas	Employment ('000)			Value added (1992 $bn)		
		1972	1992	% change	1972	1992	% change
8+	3	3,443	2,850	–17.2	215	217	1.0
4–8	6	1,972	2,408	22.1	129	205	59.4
2–4	12	1,764	2,127	20.6	113	163	44.1
1–2	19	1,790	1,971	10.1	121	169	39.8
Forty metropolitan areas	40	8,972	9,358	4.3	578	755	30.6
USA	—	19,000	18,253	–3.9	1,188	1,429	20.3

Source: US Department of Commerce, Bureau of the Census, *Census of Manufactures*, Washington, 1972 and 1992.

TABLE 4.4. Service industry receipts in the forty US metropolitan areas with a population of 1 million or more, 1992

Population category (millions)	No. of metropolitan areas	Service industry receipts (1992 $bn)		
		1972	1992	% change
8+	3	108.8	237.2	118.0
4–8	6	55.6	189.6	241.0
2–4	12	42.9	143.8	235.2
1–2	19	33.0	88.1	167.0
Forty metropolitan areas	40	240.0	658.7	174.0
USA	—	379.3	883.0	132.7

Note: The service industry is defined here (in terms of the 1987 Standard Industrial Classification) as SICs 70 (Hotels and Other Lodging Places), 72 (Personal Services), 73 (Business Services), 75 (Auto Repair, Services, and Parking), 76 (Miscellaneous Repair Services), 78 (Motion Pictures), 79 (Amusement and Recreation Services), 81 (Legal Services), 87 (Engineering and Management Services).

Source: US Department of Commerce, Bureau of the Census, *Census of Service Industries*, Washington, 1972 and 1992.

corresponding growth for the whole country over the same period was 132.7%. In 1992, a total of 74.6% of all service industry receipts in the United States was concentrated in the forty largest metropolitan areas. Over a quarter of these receipts were accounted for by New York, Los Angeles, and Chicago alone. On a global scale, the emergence of places like London, Tokyo, and Frankfurt as commanding centers of business and financial service activity offers a number of striking parallels to the US case.

One final piece of information serves to drive home the point about the tendency for economic activity to cluster in particular places. Not only are the forty largest metropolitan areas alluded to above the main foci of the US domestic economy, they are also the predominant foundation of its foreign trade efforts. In aggregate, these areas accounted for 63.5% of the total dollar value of the merchandise exports of the United States in 1994.[7] The top ten exporters were, in order, Detroit, New York, Los Angeles, Seattle, San Jose, Chicago, Houston, San Francisco, Miami, and Minneapolis, and they alone accounted for 33.8% of the US total.

Sectoral dimensions of clustering

We may ask, how do these patterns of economic location vary by sector? And what in turn can the answer to this question tell us about the basic logic of the observed trends? In providing a preliminary response to these questions, I shall again draw chiefly on empirical data for the United States, although, as later arguments will suggest, the main findings presented below can be readily generalized to other cases.

Table 4.5 provides data on the geographic clustering of manufacturing employment in the United States in 1992 by two-digit industrial sectors. For each sector, the amount of employment in the forty metropolitan areas with populations greater than 1 million is shown, together with corresponding employment levels in the United States as a whole. Also presented in the table is the percentage of employment concentrated in the forty metropolitan areas for each sector. Sectors are then ranked by these percentage values and segregated

[7] US Department of Commerce, *Metropolitan Area Exports: An Export Performance Report on over 250 US Cities*, Washington: US Department of Commerce, International Trade Administration, 1996.

TABLE 4.5. Manufacturing employment in the forty US metropolitan areas with a population of 1 million or more in 1992, by two-digit sector

Standard Industrial Category (SIC)	Employment in the forty metropolitan areas ('000)	Employment in USA ('000)	The 40 metropolitan areas as a % of the USA
Top group			
27 Printing and Publishing	922	1,506	61.2
34 Fabricated Metal Products	727	1,370	53.1
38 Instruments and Related Products	462	910	50.7
39 Miscellaneous Manufacturing Industries	178	365	48.7
36 Electronic and Other Electronic Equipment	679	1,444	47.0
30 Rubber and Miscellaneous Plastics Products	416	907	45.9
35 Industrial Machinery and Equipment	791	1,742	45.4
Middle group			
28 Chemicals and Allied Products	347	850	40.8
37 Transportation Equipment	667	1,646	40.5
23 Apparel and Other Textile Products	389	986	37.4
32 Stone, Clay, and Glass Products	175	470	37.2
25 Furniture and Fixtures	160	473	33.8
20 Food and Kindred Products	500	1,505	33.2
Bottom group			
33 Primary Metal Industries	216	663	32.6
29 Petroleum and Coal Products	36	114	31.8
26 Paper and Allied Products	198	626	31.7
24 Lumber and Wood Products	120	658	18.2
31 Leather and Leather Products	17	101	16.5
22 Textile Mill Products	98	615	15.9
21 Tobacco Products	0	38	0.0
Totals	7,078	16,989	41.7

Note: Sectors are segregated into three groups according to the percentage of their employment concentrated in the forty metropolitan areas. The designated totals are less than those in Table 4.3 because 1.26 million (unallocated) administrative and auxiliary employees have not been included in the national figures presented here.

Source: US Department of Commerce, Bureau of the Census, *Census of Manufactures*, Washington, 1992.

into three equal-sized partitions. Characteristic sectors of the group with high levels of employment concentration in the forty metropolitan areas are SIC 27 (Printing and Publishing) and SIC 36 (Electronic and Other Electronic Equipment). Characteristic sectors of the second group are SIC 37 (Transportation Equipment) and SIC 23 (Apparel and Other Textile Products); both of these sectors, it may be noted, break down into finer categories, some of which are highly concentrated and some of which are highly dispersed. The third group, with low levels of employment concentration, may be exemplified by SIC 33 (Primary Metal Industries) and SIC 26 (Paper and Allied Products). An attempt was made to isolate some of the specific factors underlying these differentials by means of logistic regression.

Logistic regression is a technique for correlating a dependent variable whose values range between zero and one (and which are thus probabilities or proportions) with any set of independent variables, where the results are such as to guarantee that predicted values of the dependent variable will always remain within their pre-defined numerical range. In the present instance, the dependent variable is defined as the ratio of (*a*) employment in the forty largest metropolitan areas to (*b*) employment in the USA as a whole; observations on this variable are represented by the two-digit SIC categories given in Table 4.5. Out of many independent variables that were examined in a preliminary round of investigation, three were isolated for further scrutiny:

1. the capital–labor ratio, i.e. the ratio of fixed capital assets to total employment;
2. average size of establishment, i.e. total employment divided by number of establishments;
3. production workers as a proportion of all employees.

These three variables are expressed in terms of aggregate national data, with all observations again being represented by two-digit SIC categories.

The results of the logistic regression are laid out in Table 4.6, along with those of a second analysis to be alluded to later. Both the capital–labor ratio and production workers as a proportion of all workers turn out to be highly significant variables, whereas average size of establishment is non-significant in statistical terms.[8] The signs

---

[8] Levels of colinearity between the three independent variables examined here are extremely small.

TABLE 4.6. Summary results of logistic regression analysis of locational clustering in two-digit manufacturing sectors and four-digit clothing industry sectors[a]

Variable	Two-digit manufacturing sectors[b]		Four-digit clothing industry sectors[c]	
	Coefficient	t-value	Coefficient	t-value
Capital–labor ratio	−0.0012	2.01	−0.1565	3.58
Average size of establishment	−0.0023	0.88	−0.0073	2.03
Production workers as a proportion of all employees	−4.2850	4.59	−3.7228	0.83
Constant term			−0.3623	−0.3236
R^2			0.59	0.46
Number of observations			19	29

Notes

[a] Both analyses apply to US data for 1992. The form of the regressions is representable as $p = a(\exp\Sigma b_i X_i)/(1 + a\exp\Sigma b_i X_i)$, where p is the proportion of employees in a given sector to be found in clustered formation (as defined in the text), X_i is the ith independent variable, and a and b_i are computed parameters.

[b] SIC 21 (Tobacco Products) is omitted from the analysis (i.e. $p_{SIC\ 21} = 0$).

[c] SICs 2381 (Fabric Dress and Work Gloves) and 2385 (Waterproof Outerwear) are omitted from the analysis (i.e. $p_{SIC\ 2381} = 0$ and $p_{SIC\ 2385} = 0$).

attached to the regression coefficients for all three independent variables are negative. Thus, as the capital–labor ratio and production workers relative to all employees fall in value in any two-digit standard industrial category, predicted locational patterns will shift from being comparatively dispersed to comparatively clustered. These results are broadly consistent with a preliminary explanation of the phenomenon of industrial clustering and dispersal as a twofold relation based on labor-intensive, unstandardized, and relatively skilled production activities in the one case, and routinization and deskilling in the other.[9]

In turn, and anticipating some of the arguments to be developed at a later stage, we might hazard the interpretation that clustering tends to ensue, *ceteris paribus*, wherever we find industries that face unstable markets whose contestability is focused mainly on product quality and innovativeness rather than cost, and dispersal wherever we find the opposite. The crudeness of definition of the variables used here, however, impedes us from making more precise statements about causalities at this stage. As it is, the computed R^2 for this analysis is a very significant 0.59.

Despite these encouraging results, the fact that they are based on such a small and heterogeneous number of observations is an inducement to look for further confirmation of the trends identified. One possible option here might be to try to replicate the same results over a larger number of more disaggregated industrial sectors. Unfortunately, we meet a serious obstacle if we simply expand the logistic regression model so as to accommodate, say, all three- or four-digit manufacturing sectors. If we proceed in this manner, it turns out that the extreme idiosyncrasy of the individual sectors (an idiosyncrasy that is in some degree masked by aggregation at higher levels of resolution) makes it difficult to extract any systematic conclusions. A way around this problem was sought by restricting the examination to four-digit sectors classified under SIC 23 (Apparel and Textile Products). This particular option offers a set of observational units that are all reasonably comparable in terms of their general structure while also being sufficiently numerous to permit trenchant statistical inference. One practical problem in using such fine sectoral definitions

---

[9] P. R. Blackley and D. Greytak, 'Competitive advantage and industrial location: an intrametropolitan evaluation', *Urban Studies*, 23 (1986): 221–30; B. Bluestone and B. Harrison, *The Deindustrialization of America*, New York: Basic Books, 1982; A. J. Scott, 'Locational patterns and dynamics of industrial activity in the modern metropolis: a review essay', *Urban Studies*, 19 (1982): 111–42.

is that the confidentiality rules that apply to information published in the US *Census of Manufactures* mean that many relevant pieces of data are simply not available, particularly for the cases of all but the very largest metropolitan areas. Accordingly, the dependent variable is now simply re-expressed as the proportion of aggregate employment located in New York and Los Angeles for each four-digit clothing industry sector. These two metropolitan areas dominate the entire US clothing industry, with just about one-fifth of all employment in SIC 23 between them. The independent variables are nominally the same as in the previous analysis, but now of course defined for four-digit clothing industry sectors.

The results of this second logistic regression analysis are laid out on the right-hand side of Table 4.6. This time the statistically significant independent variables are the capital–labor ratio and the average size of establishment, while production workers relative to total employment is non-significant, possibly because its generally high values across all four-digit clothing industry SICs reduce its powers of statistical discrimination. All variables again have an inverse impact on the dependent variable. These findings run fairly parallel to those of the first logistic regression, and can be interpreted in much the same way. However, the now significant role of the establishment size variable calls for some supplementary commentary. Falling values of the latter variable, like those of the capital–labor ratio, are a symptom of increased clustering in the clothing industry, a circumstance that can be accounted for partly by the fact that vertically disintegrated and fashion-oriented producers (who favor smaller establishments) tend to gravitate to locations close to the centers of New York and Los Angeles.[10] By contrast, large (and relatively capital-intensive) manufacturing plants making cheap factory clothing in long runs are more commonly found at dispersed locations where cheap land and labor are available.

As limited as the above analyses may be, they provide us with some preliminary insights into the dynamics of locational clustering and dispersal in modern production systems. These insights will be reworked in some theoretical detail in the next chapter, where I shall attempt to demonstrate that locational clustering is associated above

---

[10] A. J. Scott, 'Industrial organization and the logic of intra-metropolitan location, III: A case study of the women's dress industry in the Greater Los Angeles Region', *Economic Geography*, 60 (1984): 3–27.

all with transactions-intensive, labor-intensive production sectors with high endogenous levels of entrepreneurial and innovative energy. It is not difficult to deduce (and the discussion in the next chapter will make the point more clear) that these sorts of attributes are also liable to vary in inverse relation to capital–labor ratios, average establishment size, and the relative weight of production workers in total employment. The same remark is suggestively reinforced by the data presented in Tables 4.3 and 4.4, which show that services are very much more spatially concentrated than manufacturing in the United States.

Toward the idea of agglomeration

The geography of industrial and service development, then, displays a widespread proclivity to locational clustering in the form of dense polarized complexes of producers on the landscape. Since production always requires human labor, these complexes are necessarily also the sites of large masses of population and local labor-market activity, together with dependent retail and service functions.

Henceforward, I shall refer to the logic that induces these states of centripetal convergence as a spatio-temporal dynamic of *agglomeration*, and I shall develop an analysis in the next chapter that seeks to understand the bases of and the limits to this dynamic in terms of *agglomeration economies and diseconomies*. The key moment of this logic revolves around the status of any economic system as a polarized complex of interrelated production and labor-market activities as indistinctly but definitely suggested in the discussion of the logistic regression results set out in Table 4.6.

FORMS OF REGIONAL DEVELOPMENT

The productive and competitive capabilities of regions

Even in the nineteenth century it was evident that the large and specialized industrial agglomerations observable in various parts of Europe and North America could be accounted for only partially by reference to the pre-given distribution of natural endowments. The presence or otherwise of resources like coal or iron ore or natural harbors most certainly influenced the location of industry, but the spatial pattern of many sectors, such as cotton spinning and weaving in and around Manchester, or shoes and leather in the towns of southern New England, seemed at best only tenuously related to a set of underlying physical conditions. They were, to be sure, associated with pools of skilled and habituated labor, but were these pools of labor a cause or an effect of industrial development?

In the twentieth century, the gap between the geographic distribution of natural endowments and the observable shape of the economic landscape is even more pronounced. There is virtually nothing in the early history or geography of places like Detroit, Silicon Valley, or Seattle that would enable one to foretell their subsequent emergence as major world centers of the car, computer, and aircraft industries, respectively. Even in the celebrated cases of the aerospace and motion picture industries of Southern California, whose presence in the region is commonly ascribed to local climatic conditions, physically based explanations dissolve away on closer scrutiny in favor of more social constructivist accounts.[11]

Any attempt to comprehend exactly what does come to pass in these sorts of cases calls at the outset for a systematic theoretical account of both the static and dynamic logic of agglomeration. What we can say at this stage is that much economic development in the modern world is actually generated in the context of wholesale locational agglomeration, combined with specific kinds of social and political processes that shore up *regional productive and competitive capabilities*. In the most successful cases, the result is a constant stream of localized increasing-returns effects, which then often become locked in via a process of hysteresis.[12] What this means, in general, is that the many overlapping sub-systems (social divisions of labor, technologies, bodies of know-how, employment practices, reputation effects, etc.) into which regional economic complexes typically decompose all develop and grow in mutual interaction with one

[11] A. J. Scott, *Technopolis: High-Technology Industry and Regional Development in Southern California*, Berkeley and Los Angeles: University of California Press, 1993; M. Storper and S. Christopherson, 'Flexible specialization and regional industrial agglomerations: the case of the US motion picture industry', *Annals of the Association of American Geographers*, 77 (1987): 104–7.

[12] W. B. Arthur, 'Silicon Valley locational clusters: when do increasing returns imply monopoly?' *Mathematical Social Sciences*, 19 (1990): 235–51. P. A. David, 'Clio and the economics of QWERTY', *American Economic Review*, 75 (1985): 332–7; M. Porter, *The Competitive Advantage of Nations*, New York: Free Press; P. M. Romer, 'Increasing returns and long-run growth', *Journal of Political Economy*, 94 (1986): 1002–37.

another, so that their competitive powers—taken as a whole—are almost always greater than the sum of the individual competitive powers residing within each firm. The rule of Ricardian comparative advantage still remains an important key to any understanding of the ways in which regional economies become specialized and integrated into wider networks of trade, but the foundations of this process nowadays tend to be rooted in historically accumulated social and political structures rather than in raw natural endowments.

Fordist and post-fordist regions

These overarching conditions of regional development are of course realized in a great diversity of concrete geographical and historical circumstances. One distinctive expression of them is to be seen in the Manufacturing Belt of the United States (and in its geographical homologue in north-west Europe) in the decades following World War 1, with Chicago and Detroit as its chief exemplars, where a hugely successful fordist mass-production system was creating the basis of the American Dream. Yet another expression is discernible today in selected parts of North America (e.g. the Sunbelt), Western Europe (e.g. southern Germany and north-east and central Italy), and east and south-east Asia (the four tigers, and much of Japan), where dense urban and regional development has occurred in response to a later, post-fordist mode of industrialization.[13]

Fordist industrialization between about 1920 and 1965 was based more than anything else on propulsive growth pole sectors marked by powerful internal economies of scale. In its archetypal embodiment it consisted of industries like cars, machinery, domestic appliances, etc., which, together with their associated constellations of direct and indirect input suppliers, generated massive urban and regional concentrations of capital and labor as exemplified by the classic North American manufacturing metropolis.

Fordist industry was by no means the only or even perhaps the most common kind of manufacturing activity to be found in the main industrial regions of North America and Western Europe at this time, but it was at the forefront of national economic growth, and its

---

[13] A. J. Scott, 'Industrial urbanism in Southern California: post-fordist civic dilemmas and opportunities', *Contention*, 5 (1995): 39–65.

trajectory of development was widely considered to define an ideal model that virtually all other industries were expected to follow as they yielded to the imperative of technological progress.[14] It also certainly constituted most of the dynamic functional core of the great growth centers of the inter-war and post-war years, where its unique employment structure was characteristically re-expressed in the social space of the city in terms of a pervasive twofold split between blue-collar and white-collar neighborhoods. At the same time, these growth centers came to function as the nuclei of an evolving intra-national core–periphery system of regional development which probably attained to its prime spatial expression some time in the 1960s.

The beginnings of the ebb-tide of fordist mass production and the ascent of post-fordist industry as a leading edge in capitalist development can be dated from the late 1960s and early 1970s. At this time, processes of growth, technological innovation, and labor-market formation were starting decisively to be restructured as large numbers of post-fordist and flexible-production sectors in both manufacturing and service industries rose to the fore. Simultaneously, a window of locational opportunity seemed to open up as firms in these sectors sought out very different kinds of urban and regional milieus from those that had taken shape in the older industrial spaces of North America and Western Europe. This was a moment when the established pattern of industrial geography in the more developed parts of the world was undergoing severe ruptures and when a disparate group of new industrial spaces was beginning to loom into being.

In spite of the variety of locations in which these new industrial spaces are found, they almost all share the common feature that they offer social and cultural environments which are distant in functional and/or spatial terms from those that were formed and consolidated in given places under the regime of fordist mass-production industry. Above all, their political atmospheres are relatively untainted by the predispositions and traditions that pervaded the classical American and European urbanized working classes in their mid-century heyday, with their peculiar attitudes and habits, their historical self-consciousness, and their experience of organized and sustained opposition to management.

By the same token, these new industrial spaces tend to offer only limited resistance to the construction of alternative sorts of social and

---

[14] D. A. Hounshell, *From the American System to Mass Production, 1800–1932*, Baltimore: Johns Hopkins University Press, 1984.

cultural environments more appropriate to post-fordist species of production. We find them in areas like the US Sunbelt, where new high-technology industries flourish in places like Silicon Valley, Orange County, or Austin; in the traditional urban centers of north-east and central Italy, with their profusion of high-grade craft industries; in the major cities of east and south-east Asia, with their enormously diverse economic bases focused especially on many different kinds of electronics and craft industries; and in global cities like New York, London, Frankfurt, Paris, or Tokyo, where much of the command, control, financial, and cultural functions of the modern world economy are concentrated.

Important aspects of this still-evolving historical–geographical conjuncture can be discerned in the changing economic fortunes of the US Frostbelt and Sunbelt since the early 1970s. Recall from Table 4.3 that manufacturing employment in the forty largest metropolitan areas of the United States grew by 4.3% between 1972 and 1992. However, when we reconstitute this information so as to reflect events in the conventional Frostbelt–Sunbelt macro-regions, we find that manufacturing employment in the metropolitan areas of the former zone declined by 12.4% over 1972–92, whereas it grew by 48.5% in the metropolitan areas of the latter. Much of this shift can be ascribed to the relative locational concentration of older fordist mass-production industries in the Frostbelt, and of newer post-fordist production sectors in the Sunbelt.

Once this has been said, industrial employment in many parts of the Frostbelt (and the Midwest in particular) are now showing signs of new growth after a long period of crisis, and as the last major relics of fordist-era industrial capacity and practices are being cleared away.[15] As this happens, flexible-production activities have been re-colonizing the voids that have been left behind. In addition, service industry employment has grown rapidly and more or less uninterruptedly in major cities throughout the country over the last few decades. Such growth has occurred even in Frostbelt cities, where the service sector has always been quite segregated in both geographic and social terms from the old fordist manufacturing activities that were to be found there.

[15] R. Florida, 'Regional creative destruction: production organization, globalization, and the economic transformation of the Midwest', *Economic Geography*, 72 (1966): 314–34.

THE NEW WORLD MAP OF REGIONS

The economic geography of today's world is a complex palimpsest composed of locational residues from previous historical rounds of economic growth, but now being dominantly restructured by processes of post-fordist industrialization, regional development, and world-wide economic integration.

I have already noted on a number of occasions that one of the dominant features of this economic geography is a world order made up by two interlocking systems of production and exchange. On the one hand, we observe a widening structure of national and international commodity chains in which products originating in particular locations are passed on for further processing or final consumption to other locations around the world. On the other hand, we are also witnessing a state of affairs where to an increasing degree the individual nodes of these global commodity chains are constituted as dense intra-regional constellations of economic activity, with the entire set of nodes forming an irregular world-wide mosaic. The whole is imbricated within complex national variations in levels of economic opportunity and marginalization, with some countries drawing enormous benefits from the emerging new world order while others are clearly lagging behind.

A schematic outline of the world map that seems to be coming into being as these processes work themselves out is presented in Figure 4.2.

Here, the developed areas of the world are represented as a system of polarized regional economies each consisting of a central metropolitan area and a surrounding hinterland (of indefinite extent) occupied by ancillary communities, prosperous agricultural zones, smaller tributary centers, and the like. As indicated in the figure, some of these metropolis–hinterland systems may actually fuse together to form megalopolitan regions as in the actual cases of Boston–New York–Philadelphia, Los Angeles–San Diego–Tijuana, Milan–Turin–Genoa, the Dutch Randstad, Tokyo–Nagoya–Osaka, and so on. Each metropolitan nucleus is the site of intricate networks of specialized but complementary forms of economic activity, together with large, multifaceted local labor markets, and each is a locus of powerful agglomeration economies and increasing returns effects. As such, they are not only large in size but also constantly growing yet larger. These entities can be thought of as *the regional motors of the new global economy*.

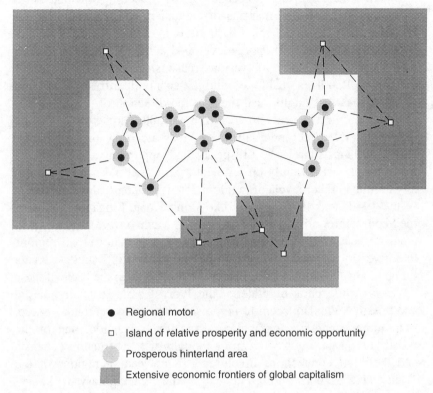

● Regional motor

□ Island of relative prosperity and economic opportunity

Prosperous hinterland area

Extensive economic frontiers of global capitalism

FIG. 4.2. A schematic representation of the contemporary geography of global capitalism

Equally, there are large expanses of the modern world that lie at the extensive economic margins of capitalism (former colonies, ex-socialist states, areas occupied by traditional cultures resistant to capitalist norms, and so on). Underdeveloped areas like these have been held back economically for various reasons, including the fact that they have often been unable to build the economic infrastructures and organizations that might push them in the direction of growth center development and hence into localized virtuous circles of economic expansion. Even so, underdeveloped areas are occasionally punctuated by islands of relative prosperity and opportunity, and some of these are almost certainly on a trajectory that will take them eventually to much higher levels of (agglomerated) economic development.[16] In the 1960s and 1970s, places like Hong Kong, Singapore, Taiwan, the Seoul metropolitan region, and central Mexico were all positioned along the early stages of this trajectory. Today, many urban regions in a diversity of newly industrializing countries (e.g. Bangkok, Kuala Lumpur, Guangzhou, and São Paulo) are following on the heels of these pioneers, while parts of Nigeria, the Ivory Coast, India, Indonesia, and possibly Vietnam seem to be poised close to the initiatory phase.

In more concrete geographical terms, the schematic map of the world laid out in Figure 4.2 can be thought of as a structure of nodes and their interconnections involving (*a*) the leading regions of the Triad countries, constituting the heart of the contemporary world system, and (*b*) a set of subsidiary geographic spaces corresponding to much of Africa, Latin America, and parts of Asia. The detailed underlying geometry of this entire structure reflects a complex past history of economic and political dependencies in which the regions of Asia are dominantly tied to Japan, those of Latin America to the United States, and those of Africa to Europe. Castells has demonstrated that this basic ossature is replicated over and over again in a wide variety of trade and investment flows in the modern world.[17]

With the passage of time, this world-wide system of regions will predictably become steadily more tightly bound together within an overarching division of labor. On theoretical grounds, we may predict that this will be accompanied in all probability by a tendency for

---

[16] J. Agnew and S. Corbridge, *Mastering Space: Hegemony, Territory, and International Political Economy*, London: Routledge, 1995.

[17] M. Castells, *The Rise of the Network Society*, Oxford: Blackwell, 1996.

the world's regions to become yet more specialized and differentiated from one another in economic terms. The latter remark is echoed in some preliminary empirical work by Krugman and Venables, who have demonstrated that the major economic regions in the United States (which are roughly equivalent in size to individual European countries) are much more specialized in their manufacturing functions than the countries of the European Union.[18] However, with falling internal tariff barriers in the Union, thereby enlarging markets, European countries/regions now appear to be moving in the direction of more pronounced economic specialization. The newly prosperous city-states of Hong Kong and Singapore provide ample evidence that regional economic specialization (linked to export-oriented growth policies) can be an extremely successful formula for accelerated development in the global system.

THE SOCIAL ORDER OF THE MOSAIC

If capital is relatively mobile in the modern world, labor by contrast remains much more spatially confined, though assuredly not perfectly immobile. This circumstance provides an incentive for holders of capital to scour the world for very specific kinds of labor inputs in order to enhance levels of profit, while by the same token continually destabilizing the geographic outlines of the entire system.

Recall that the new international division of labor theorists based an extremely stark prediction on this state of affairs with their claims about the incipient division of the world into two interdependent but clearly unequal zones. Core countries, they suggested, were destined to become foci of top-quality managerial, professional, and technical jobs, with the periphery becoming a sort of undifferentiated low-wage, low-skill haven for the branch plants of multinational corporations. This prediction about the socio-spatial evolution of the global system has turned out in practice to be over-drawn, and actual geographic distributions of socio-economic functions to be very much more complex than the original new international division of labor thesis seemed to allow. It is true that we can speak quite meaningfully of broad

[18] P. Krugman and A. J. Venables, *Globalization and the Inequality of Nations*, Cambridge, Mass.: Bureau of Economic Research, Working Paper no. 5098, 1995.

categories of countries and regions defined in terms of their level of development, and in particular of:

1. highly developed world leaders;
2. newly industrializing or middle-income countries and regions in transitional phases of development; and
3. underdeveloped outliers and left-behinds.

However, these cases are almost always more internally differentiated than their generalized profiles suggest. There are many widespread and stubborn instances of low-wage, low-skill economic activity in highly developed parts of the world, and of skilled managerial, professional and technical employment in less developed parts of the world. Above all, and despite their notable economic successes on many fronts, the main regional motors of the global economy invariably contain large pools of low-wage jobs and marginalized unskilled workers. They are often, as a consequence, rife with problems and predicaments that germinate within the swollen underside of their labor market and social structures.

The progressive globalization of economic relations has subjected most of these motors to intense competitive and demographic pressures which have generally aggravated these dilemmas, and which simultaneously have tended to induce sharp bifurcations in local social formations. This tendency is most evident in the propensity for the economies of dense post-fordist agglomerations to split into a high-skill, high-wage employment segment on the one hand, and a low-grade segment employing large numbers of people in a diversity of sweatshop manufacturing sectors and service sectors on the other hand.[19] This pattern of social segmentation is reinforced by the intense attraction of these agglomerations for immigrants from peripheral countries and regions; witness the massive migration of Central Americans and South-east Asians to Los Angeles, Puerto Ricans and Haitians to New York, North and West Africans to Paris, and Filipino and Mainland Chinese workers to Hong Kong. The overall social segmentation that ensues engenders mounting tensions (often with racial and ethnic overtones) in these places, together with an endemic suscep-

---

[19] J. Friedmann and G. Wolff, 'World city formation: an agenda for research and action', *International Journal of Urban and Regional Research*, 6 (1982): 309–44; S. Sassen, *The Global City: London, New York, Tokyo*, Princeton: Princeton University Press, 1991; R. Waldinger and M. Bozorgmehr (eds.), *Ethnic Los Angeles*, New York: Russell Sage Foundation, 1996.

tibility to sporadic social eruptions and a persistent subversion of the latent function of the large metropolis as a gregarious community of communities. These trends have been exacerbated in the United States —nowhere more so than in the two leading cities of New York and Los Angeles—by the neo-conservative social policies that have been steadily diffusing through all levels of government since the early 1980s, and that have tended persistently to undercut the economic capacities and social welfare of those at the bottom of the employment ladder.

5

The Regional Foundations of Economic Performance

In previous chapters I have tried to lay out a broad empirical panorama of the rise and nascent consolidation of a globally interlinked network of regional economies. In order to push our understanding of these matters further forward, we now must shift into a more conceptual mode of investigation and look carefully at some basic ideas about the relations between geography and economic performance, where by 'performance' I mean growth and development as manifest in such specific variables as productivity, innovation, employment, competitiveness, and so on.

The point here is that we need both to clarify the locational logic of productive activity and to show how this logic then operates in reflexive relation to the dynamics of performance. This task involves much more than a simple rehearsal of classical location theory, which in its received versions (i.e. accounts of the spatial geometry of the economy) has always been a rather minor appendage to economic theory as a whole. The task before us here is to develop a view of location that is also a set of propositions about the necessary dependence of the economic order at large on geography. This is a task that modern economic geographers have begun to tackle with much success, and with some dramatic consequences, too, for the ways in which we can begin to think about local economic development policy.[1]

---

[1] See e.g. B. Harrison, *Lean and Mean: The Changing Landscape of Corporate Power in the Age of Flexibility*, New York: Basic Books, 1994; A. Saxenian, *Regional Advantage: Culture and Competition in Silicon Valley and Route 128*, Cambridge, Mass.: Harvard University Press, 1994; A. J. Scott, 'The geographic foundations of industrial performance', *Competition and Change*, 1 (1995): 51–66; M. Storper and R. Walker, *The Capitalist Imperative: Territory, Technology, and Industrial Growth*, Oxford: Blackwell, 1989.

INDUSTRIAL ORGANIZATION AND ECONOMIC SPACE

The structure of economic activity

There is a long tradition of economic analysis, ranging from Böhm-Bawerck[2] through Young[3] and Leontieff[4] to Perroux,[5] Isard,[6] and beyond, in which production is described as a social division of labor whose discrete nodes (i.e. individual producers or aggregates of producers) are held functionally together by extensive networks of transactions. In such a system, any producer, say A, sells a quantity of output to another producer, say B; B adds some value to the product and then sells to C; C adds further value and sells to D; and so on, until at some stage the product is taken out of the circuit of production and consumed. At any point in the circuit, some of the product can return to an earlier node for further processing; then, as the division of labor deepens and widens, we say, following Böhm-Bawerck, that the *roundaboutness* of the circuit is increasing, i.e. that the number of processing stages between raw-material inputs and the final consumer is expanding.

This descriptive model can be immediately enriched by thinking of each node in the circuit of production as an input–output mechanism such that there is a definite relation between a quantity of given input (e.g. sheet metal or plastic parts) and a quantity of derivative output (e.g. aircraft or computers). A basic condition sustaining the existence of any pre-defined division of labor is that producers can always purchase their inputs more cheaply and effectively from outside sources than they can make them themselves.

The latter remark takes us at once into questions of industrial organization as originally formulated by Coase in 1937 and Williamson in 1975, and which provide some important foundations for the integration of issues of economic location and performance.[7] In their

---

[2] E. von Böhm-Bawerck, *The Positive Theory of Capital*, New York: G. E. Stechert, 1891.

[3] A. Young, 'Increasing returns and economic progress', *Economic Journal*, 38 (1928): 527–42.

[4] W. Leontieff, *The Structure of the American Economy*, Cambridge, Mass.: Harvard University Press, 1941.

[5] F. Perroux, *L'Economie du XXᵉ Siècle*, Paris: Presses Universitaires de France, 1961.

[6] W. Isard, *Methods of Regional Analysis*, Cambridge, Mass.: MIT Press, 1960.

[7] R. H. Coase, 'The nature of the firm', *Economica*, 4 (1937): 386–405; O. E. Williamson, *Markets and Hierarchies: Analysis and Antitrust Implications*, New York: Free Press, 1975.

essence, these questions boil down to a series of theoretical propositions about the relations between firms and markets, and above all
about their *scope*, i.e. the range of interconnected types of production tasks internalized within any one system of managerial control
(the domain of the firm) versus the range and types of interconnected
firms that make up the social division of labor (the domain of the
market). When the internal scope of firms is increasing (which in a
static world means that the external scope of the market is decreasing), we say that *vertical integration* is occurring. An example of this
phenomenon is the combination of semiconductor production and
computer manufacturing into single units of production where there
are strong technological interdependencies between the two, e.g.
where their common internalization allows the free flow of technological information and know-how between them, thereby enhancing
their overall efficacy. If, by contrast, firms are shedding functions and
their internal scope is decreasing (with the external scope of the market increasing as a consequence), we say that *vertical disintegration*
is occurring. An example here might be the splitting up of cotton-
spinning and weaving functions into separate firms thus allowing
them to attain higher levels of production flexibility as represented
by more varied outputs or more frequent design changes. It should
be noted that between the domains of the firm and the market there
are many possible intermediate (quasi-internal, quasi-external) organizational states including, for example, informal agreements, written
contracts, joint ventures, partnerships, *keiretsu*-style associations, and
so on, that add a further layer of complexity to the structural fabric
of production.[8]

Coase and Williamson, together with a number of other industrial
organization theorists,[9] have provided elaborate analytical accounts of
the many and varied conditions that lead to vertical integration or disintegration of production systems. It is not necessary here to dwell on

[8] W. W. Powell, 'Neither market nor hierarchy: network forms of organization', in
B. M. Staw and L. L. Cummings (eds.), *Research in Organizational Behavior*, xii,
Greenwich, Conn.: JAI Press, 1990, pp. 295–336.

[9] See, e.g. A. A. Alchian and H. Demsetz, 'Production, information costs and economic
organization', *American Economic Review*, 62 (1972): 777–95; D. W. Carlton, 'Vertical
integration in competitive markets under uncertainty', *Journal of Industrial Economics*, 27
(1979): 189–209; J. C. Panzar and R. D. Willig, 'Economies of scope', *American Economic
Review (Papers and Proceedings)*, 71 (1981): 46–58; D. J. Teece, 'Economies of scope
and the scope of the enterprise', *Journal of Economic Organization and Behavior*, 1
(1986): 223–47.

the details of these accounts except to observe that a calculus of transactions costs tends to play a significant role in their analytical machinery. We may observe too, following Granovetter and others, that a strictly economic logic of production will take us only so far in understanding industrial organization processes, and that we need also to take into account the fact that transactional systems are always and of necessity embedded in historically determinate social conditions.[10] Thus, in the example of semiconductor production and computer manufacturing cited above, it is possible that vertical integration might be deferred or only partially implemented if social conditions were such as to promote high levels of trust between firms, thus permitting requisite flows of information to occur without formal amalgamation. In any case, a given economic system will always be constituted as a complex network of relatively integrated and relatively disintegrated firms in a constant state of adjustment and readjustment as shifts in technologies, labor markets, the competitive environment, and so on occur.

Any social division of labor (whether defined in terms of sectors or firms) can be thought of as defining an *economic space* in which every firm or sector, as the case may be, has an explicit input–output relationship to all other firms or sectors. We must distinguish this notion of economic space from the notion of *geographic space*, which represents a locus of actual places, whether functionally interrelated with one another or not. Economic space itself can assume many different structural forms, though two archetypes are of some relevance to the present discussion. One of these is represented by pyramid-like industrial complexes where large lead plants (often possessing a wide scope of internalized production activities) sit at the top of transactional hierarchies of smaller input suppliers, service providers, and subcontractors (see Figure 5.1). This polarized organizational form is typical of the car or aerospace industries. The other involves finely grained transactional networks linking together many small and vertically disintegrated producers, without the strong centralization effects that are to be found in the former case. This type is exemplified by industries such as clothing, jewelry, or advanced semiconductor manufacturing (see Figure 5.2). Many different sorts of hybrid or amorphous expressions of economic space are possible too. Whatever their specific

---

[10] M. Granovetter, 'Economic action and social structure: the problem of embeddedness', *American Journal of Sociology*, 91 (1985): 481–510.

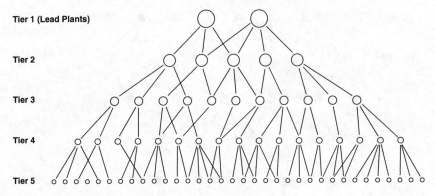

FIG. 5.1. A pyramid-like economic space

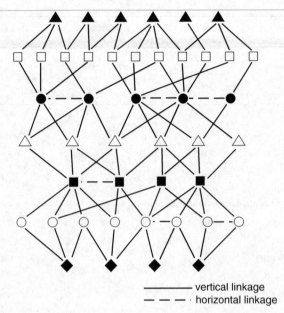

FIG. 5.2. A diffuse economic space with vertical and horizontal linkages

geometric outlines, they all represent structures of economic inter-dependence held together by an organic social division of labor.

Externalities

By the same token, economic space is also the site of numerous exter-nalities which impose definite benefits and costs on individual pro-ducers. An externality is any occurrence or activity that lies outside the range of control of the individual firm, but that then has definite effects on the firm's internal production function. Some externalities are internalized by firms through normal market channels, as for example when a firm buys inputs from another firm that can produce them to a higher standard of tolerance than it can itself achieve. Other externalities—and these are among the most interesting ones from our standpoint—are prone to market failures of various kinds and thus are not subject to the logic of the pricing system. These exter-nalities may be either positive (e.g. information spill-overs that sup-ply useful knowledge *gratis* to firms that did not participate in its creation) or negative (e.g. air pollution, or cheap imitators of a fash-ion trend that then becomes quickly debased). Many kinds of exter-nalities exhibit increasing returns effects. This means that the more abundant they are, the more beneficial in proportional terms they become (if positive) or detrimental (if negative) to the firms that inter-nalize them.

Of all the many and various externalities that exist in any production system, some of the most potent derive from the fact that economic space is by definition a domain of exchange, interaction, and flow. It can be represented not only as a field of physical input–output trans-actions between producers, but also as a gigantic never-ending multi-way discussion in which individual economic agents exchange, barter, deal, dispense instructions, learn from one another, come to know and to understand one another, and in general keep the wheels of com-merce fully greased. It is, in short, a social and interpersonal as much as an economic network in the narrow sense.

For example, the innovative capacities of individual producers are frequently much enhanced by the bits and pieces of information that circulate informally and continuously through economic space. Sign-ificant elements of this kind of information, of course, represent so much floating chaff, but some of it has surprisingly stimulating and beneficial repercussions on economic activity. Thus, as both von Hippel and Russo have indicated, a dialogue between a supplier and a buyer about a particular order and its specifications—especially where mismatches between the supplier's initial capabilities and the buyer's initial demands become apparent—can often lead to innovative insights, e.g. on the one side about how process configurations might be improved, and on the other about how alternative product designs might be put more effectively to work.[11] This type of innovation almost always entails small-scale, informal, day-by-day refinements of processes and products, and it needs to be distinguished from the kinds of innovation that come from large-scale research efforts associated with aprioristic projects like the quest for space satellites, supercomputers, effective batteries for electric cars, and so on. Nevertheless, the cumulative effect of these small refinements over time can often be enormous, and will usually be most intense where economic interdependencies are strongly developed.

Another major type of externality that is closely dependent on the transactional structure of production concerns the formation of peculiar cultural niches in certain articulations of economic space. In view of the high levels of interaction and interdependence among groups of individuals caught up in particular constellations of productive activity, they often acquire distinctive social perceptions, understandings, attitudes, and even vocabularies. Specific styles of competition and collaboration, tacit social agreements between different parties (e.g. management and labor), common frames of reference for judging reputations or trustworthiness—all are susceptible to construction in this manner. In many instances, as Salais and Storper have written, we can think of these phenomena as conventions, for even when they are not explicitly formalized, they are often represented by indurated habits, rituals, and ideologies that guide human action in predictable directions and that have forceful impacts on business operations in both positive and negative ways.[12] Segments of the economy such as electronics manufacturing, financial services, or the film industry are all heavily marked by traits of this sort, and we can properly think

---

[11] E. Von Hippel, *The Sources of Innovation*, New York: Oxford University Press, 1988; M. Russo, 'Technical change and the industrial district: the role of interfirm industrial relations in the growth and transformation of ceramic tile production in Italy', *Research Policy*, 14 (1985): 329–43.

[12] R. Salais and M. Storper, *Les Mondes de Production: Enquête sur l'Identité Economique de la France*, Paris: Editions de l'Ecole des Hautes Etudes en Sciences Sociales, 1993.

of these segments as distinctive cultural milieux, though the reader must again be reminded that the discussion is still focused on economic and not geographic space. Indeed, Marshall's celebrated though by now heavily overworked dictum about 'industrial atmosphere' and its constitution as an overarching structure of useful customs and sensitivities[13] can be interpreted in the first instance and in notional terms as a placeless and strictly sectoral phenomenon adhering to purely functional communities of producers.

The spatiality of transactions

This description of the structure of economic space and the externalities that are interwoven with it highlights the critical importance of transactions in the everyday functioning of production systems. Transactions are in part an outcome of the division of labor and the resulting inter-firm flows of inputs and outputs. But they also function as channels of social communication, and, as just demonstrated, they are one of the bases of reproducible forms of cultural solidarity.

At the same time, transactions have a dual dimensionality. They exist not only in economic space but in geographic space as well. They are therefore marked by attributes of location and distance, meaning that they are stretched out between sets of origins and destinations, and that they accordingly incur various costs as the space between these locations is spanned. This signifies in turn that mutual locational proximity (i.e. in geographic space) of firms that are interlinked in economic space is often highly beneficial to all parties. The degree of benefit, however, is intimately dependent on a number of critical qualitative features of the transactional system, as indicated in the following three points.

First, very small-scale transactions, in which the value of what is being transacted is low *relative to* its spatially dependent costs (e.g. a small-batch order from a clothing manufacturer to a sewing subcontractor), will in general be economical only over short distances. Larger transactions enjoy economies of scale that make it possible to stretch them out over much longer distances.

Second, transactions that are continually changing in their specifications and are irregular in space and time are likely to be associated

---

[13] A. Marshall, *Principles of Economics*, London: Macmillan, 1919.

with high space-dependent costs. More standardized, streamlined, and predictable transactions can take advantage of significant savings in ordering, scheduling, packaging, investment in dedicated transportation facilities, and so on, thus allowing for more spatially extensive links. Firms that depend on irregular kinds of transaction often locate in dense and multifaceted agglomerations because the external economies of scope in such areas provide insurance against unpredictable eventualities.

Third, different modes of transacting have very different implications for spatially dependent costs. For example, face-to-face encounters, where two or more individuals must come together at a single location in order to deliberate over some exchange, are typically very costly. By contrast, the electronic transmission of messages is easily accomplished over even intercontinental distances.

A rough corollary of these three points is that firms whose transactions with one another are small in scale, irregular and unpredictable, and dependent on intensive face-to-face intervention will probably find it to their advantage to be located in some sort of mutual proximity, whereas firms whose transactions with one another have the opposite characteristics are likely to be more free in their choices of location.

Critics of the transactions-cost approach to location theory have sometimes claimed that it is too narrowly focused on the monetary costs attached to the physical transportation of finished and semi-finished outputs. In actuality, spatially dependent transactions costs refer to any kind of geographic impediment to any kind of interaction (from the most concrete to the most insubstantial) between locations, including purely social and psychological evaluations of interlinkage. The point, however, is that space (or distance) is always fundamentally present as a barrier to be crossed. Even the purely monetary costs of transacting are highly multidimensional. Thus, in addition to being measured on a simple direct transport cost scale, they may also be measured in terms of personnel travel time, rates of deterioration of materials or information, velocities of circulation of inputs and outputs, the efficacity of just-in-time production systems, and so on. Moreover, these costs, in the widest sense of the term, apply to both traded and untraded forms of interdependency between individual transactors, whether we are talking about the transmission of train-loads of coal or about social encounters over lunch. Even in a world of advanced electronic communications technologies enabling some kinds of information to flow across the globe virtually without any time lag and at trivial monetary expense, geographic space still exerts major restraints on many kinds of transacting. This state of affairs will continue until such time as we have the equivalent of magic carpets, which is to say instantaneous and costless transmission of all goods and services (including labor services) in any quantity from any point in the world to any other point, on command.

THE GENERAL THEORY OF LOCATION

These remarks take us at once into the central questions of modern location theory, that is how and why different types of production occur at different levels of quantitative resolution in different places, and how any specific locational outcome affects the performative qualities of the economy.

Classical location theory has a long and intellectually rich history, ranging from the early formulations of Alfred Weber about cost-minimizing strategies for locating individual plants, through the central-place constructs of Christaller and Lösch, to the general spatial equilibrium analytics of the regional science school in the 1960s and 1970s.[14] Much of classical location theory examines the effects of physical transportation costs on individual locational decision-making and behavior, and then seeks to calculate the resulting geometric layout of the economic landscape. More recently, theorists of the so-called 'new economic geography' approach have sought to re-express location theory in terms of what we might call a historical–structural agenda. In this agenda (to be developed more fully later), the rationality of individual decision-making and behavior is subsumed within the analysis of locational patterns as the expression of spatial and temporal interdependencies in which collective effects like agglomeration,

[14] A. Weber, *Theory of the Location of Industries*, trans. C. J. Friedrich, Chicago: University of Chicago Press, 1929; W. Christaller, *Die Zentralen Orte in Süddeutschland*, Jena: Fischer, 1933, trans. C. Baskin, *The Central Places of Southern Germany*, Englewood Cliffs, NJ: Prentice-Hall, 1966; A. Lösch, *Die Räumliche Ordnung der Wirtschaft*, Jena: Fischer, 1941, trans. W. H. Woglom and W. F. Stolper, *The Economics of Location*, New Haven: Yale University Press, 1954; W. Isard, *Location and Space Economy*, Cambridge, Mass.: MIT Press, 1956.

institutional frameworks, and system-wide path dependency are allowed their full play.[15]

We can begin the task of developing these ideas more fully (but without abandoning completely certain critical insights of classical location theory) by looking at the interrelations between transactions costs, externalities, and location under a series of controlled conceptual conditions. In this exercise, I shall restrict the notion of transactions costs to spatially dependent phenomena, i.e. costs that vary solely as distance varies; and I shall deal only with those kinds of *unpriced* externalities that are generated by the co-existence of multiple firms. Recall that such externalities often engender marked increasing returns effects.

If we combine these two variables in various degrees of intensity, we observe a series of theoretical locational results as presented in Table 5.1. Notice that the table has one more column than rows in order to accommodate the special and extremely important case where spatially dependent transactions costs are heterogeneous in the sense that they are low for some kinds of interaction and high for others.

We may examine the contents of the table by looking at each of its numbered panels in turn. The reader is warned that the following discussion is intended to be illustrative rather than analytically definitive, and it is in particular abstracted away from any historical context or developmental logic. Moreover, it should be kept in mind that transactional relationships and externalities are not, strictly speaking, independent of one another, for the former commonly provide channels through which access to the latter is obtained (as in the celebrated example of the apple orchard that supplies nectar to bees, while the bees pollinate the apple blossoms; however, the bees must transport themselves from the hive to the orchard and back again).

1. *Low transactions costs, low externalities.* As spatially dependent transactions costs fall, we approach closer and closer to a state of the world represented by the magic-carpets analogy; and with

---

[15] G. Becattini (ed.), *Mercato e Forzi Locali: Il Distretto Industriale*, Bologna: Il Mulino, 1987; A. J. Scott and P. Cooke, 'The new geography and sociology of production', *Environment and Planning D: Society and Space*, 6 (1988): 241–4; E. W. Soja, R. Morales, and G. Wolff, 'Urban restructuring: an analysis of social and spatial change in Los Angeles', *Economic Geography*, 59 (1983): 195–230; M. Storper, *The Regional World: Territorial Development in a Global Economy*, New York: Guilford, 1997.

TABLE 5.1. Schematic locational outcomes resulting from the combination of spatially dependent transactions costs and externalities

Externalities	Spatially dependent transactions costs		
	Uniformly low	Heterogeneous	Uniformly high
Low	1. Spatial entropy	2. Random dispersal combined with emerging Löscherian–Weberian landscapes	3. Löscherian–Weberian landscapes
High	4. Small interconnected clusters	5. Super-clusters	6. Small disconnected clusters

falling externalities (as defined), firms' performance levels become increasingly independent of one another. In the theoretically limiting case, where all transactions costs are absolutely zero (and even where positive externalities are present), full spatial entropy, i.e. locational randomness, will prevail.

2. *Heterogeneous transactions costs, low externalities.* In situations where some transactions costs are low and others high while externalities remain at a consistently low level, we are likely to encounter a hybrid situation represented by some random dispersal of locations combined with emerging Löschian–Weberian landscapes (see next paragraph).

3. *High transactions costs, low externalities.* Under these conditions, locational patterns will be uniformly and responsively structured by the effects of distance. This suggests that producers will tend to seek out locations that reduce transport costs on inputs and outputs to the lowest possible level, and/or provide optimal access to markets over a given spatial range. Since externalities are negligible, firms will be locationally indifferent to one another except insofar as they are connected by input–output relations. The concrete geographical structures that are apt to ensue may be described as either (*a*) Löschian central-place systems, or (*b*) Weberian landscapes characterized by an irregular but cost-minimizing distribution of producers reflecting underlying patterns of resource availability, input–output linkages, and the locations of final markets.

4. *Low transactions costs, high externalities.* As we shift from panel 1 in Table 5.1 to panel 4 (i.e. from low to high externalities in the context of uniformly low transactions costs), we are likely to begin to observe the formation of small production clusters made up of firms that generate particularly intense positive externalities for one another. These clusters will remain small since the low transactions costs make it possible for inter-firm linkages and externality effects to occur over long distances, thus eliminating the need for proximity except on a very selective basis. Under these circumstances, for example, one might imagine parts of the Hollywood film industry breaking up into geographically detached but strongly interacting sub-clusters each based on a specialized trade such as scenario writing, special effects, animation, photographic processing, film shooting, and so on.

5. *Heterogeneous transactions costs, high externalities.* This case is actually the most crucial one for the purposes of the discussion in

this book, and I shall argue that the current moment of economic geography and history is one that is precisely described by the boundary conditions here, namely (*a*) spatially dependent transactions costs that range, for example, from the minuscule for international currency exchanges to onerous for many kinds of face-to-face encounters, and (*b*) high externalities, especially in the case of post-fordist flexible production systems. In the latter kinds of systems, most notably those marked by advanced levels of vertical disintegration, producers frequently cluster tightly together, both because a significant proportion of their mutual transactions incur high costs, and because the externalities that they jointly engender are copious. Yet at the same time, low costs on selected extra-local transactions enable each cluster to tap into world-wide resources and markets, thus stimulating massive local growth. Under the right combination of circumstances, the result can be the emergence of a large number of different super-clusters of capital and labor.

6. *High transactions costs, high externalities.* The solution proposed in the final panel of Table 5.1 is similar to that of panel 4, in that the prevailing locational pattern consists of small clusters, but with the difference that they are here relatively disconnected from one another. Actually, under the severe—indeed, strictly imaginary—analytical assumptions of a world that has no prior history and no geographic variations in basic resource availability, the trend would now be toward the emergence of one large agglomeration of producers. A more probable outcome, however, would be the case where we observe many small clusters, each with well-developed intra-cluster externalities, and each being located in relation to some antecedent condition of development or resource availability (as in the example of pre-capitalist craft communities). However, the high transactions costs will make it economically difficult for firms to engage with each other over extended distances, and this will therefore impose strict limits on any one cluster's ability to grow.

These schematic comments provide us with a rough preliminary sense of the potential complexity of locational outcomes, even when the basic framework conditions governing them are limited to just a few variations in transactions costs and externalities. Needless to say, this complexity is enormously increased if we append other conditions to the framework in order to take account of wider historical, social, and cultural forces. The argument that is in course of development in these chapters advances the thesis that in the current conjuncture the peculiar substantive thrust of the latter forces greatly intensifies the tendency for super-clusters to emerge. In this conjuncture, very significant elements of the production system are concentrated in locational magnets which draw their centripetal vigor from their abundant externalities combined with selectively high transactions costs; yet simultaneously, many of the goods and services that they produce flow with ease across the face of the earth. It is in this sense that we can speak of locational constraints on the globalization of production systems, even while the globalization of markets proceeds apace around us.[16]

In passing, we may observe that a complementary phenomenon to super-clusters is the rising tide of temporary agglomeration phenomena formed by the episodic build-up of externality effects leading to brief but intense congregations of many individuals in particular places. Examples are events such as business conventions, trade fairs, scientific congresses, and so on. In such cases, participants from widely scattered locations come together for short periods of time in order to engage in information exchange, discussion and debate, renewal of personal contact, and collective action.

The regional motors of the global economy can be likened to the theoretical super-clusters described above. As political barriers to economic interaction continue to fade, these motors may be expected to become, at least for a time, an overwhelmingly dominant element of the world system. I submit that we are poised at the early stages of the rise of a global economic order characterized by just such a set of regional motors as this. This claim is all the more emphatic because many of these motors are in practice made up of intersecting and overlapping (but distinctive) industrial sub-systems that usually help to boost the total local stock of agglomeration economies to yet higher levels than would obtain under conditions of strictly mono-industrial development. Although small and medium-sized clusters of economic activity thrive in huge numbers throughout the modern world, the current situation is one in which the incidence and size of super-clusters are also clearly on the increase.

[16] M. Storper, 'The limits to globalization: technology districts and international trade', *Economic Geography*, 68 (1992): 60–93; see also J. M. de Vet, 'Globalisation and local and regional competitiveness', *STI Review*, no. 13 (1993): 89–122.

THE SPECIFIC THEORY OF LOCATIONAL AGGLOMERATION

These last remarks call for further substantiation, and above all for further elaboration in terms of a specific theory of spatial agglomeration. The discussion now proceeds on two main fronts. First, I lay out some essentials of a purely static and transactional approach to understanding agglomeration. Second, I develop a story about the dynamics of agglomeration processes, paying particular attention to the path dependency and emergent effects of regional production complexes.

The static transactional theory

Any economic or social system can always be decomposed, at one level, into a dense criss-crossing network of transactional relationships. Such relationships are the essential foundation, even if they are not the totality, of all varieties of human interaction. They sustain the social division of labor, they are one of the bases of local labor markets, they function as the indispensable scaffolding of social and cultural routines, they are integral to the dissemination of many types of externality. And, precisely because they are spatially extensive and hence incur spatially dependent economic and social costs, they play a major role in the structuring of locational events.

At an earlier stage, I showed how the costs of transacting across geographic space vary enormously depending not just on distance, but also on the quantitative, technical, and social attributes of the transactional system. Wherever these costs are high, especially where there exist dense articulations of transactions in economic space, there is always some reasonable expectation of finding that the firms involved will be located in close proximity to one another in geographic space. We would in the first instance expect agglomeration to be fairly prominently developed in the case of highly disintegrated production systems, whose associated transactional networks are typified by many small transactions which are constantly changing in terms of their content and destinations, and which also require labor-intensive techniques of mediation. In addition, once proximity between producers is established, the rate of flow of circulating capital can be greatly accelerated, and the production schedules of interrelated firms can be more finely calibrated. In the Japanese *kanban* system, for example, mutual proximity of participant firms is commonly (though by no means invariably) needed for the system to work effectively. Any agglomeration of the sort under discussion here, then, will almost always be constituted as a collection of specialized but complementary economic activities held together by labyrinthine, high-cost transactional networks, and above all reinforced by the many increasing-returns effects that come into being as agglomerations form.

Labor is also, and of necessity, an element of any such system, and any tendency to agglomeration will be further enhanced by the local labor-market structures that always take shape around any center of production. This remark raises intricate questions that cannot in any sense be adequately dealt with in the present account, and only a brief sketch of some preliminary ideas will be attempted.[17] These ideas are all related to the initial observation that the daily journey to work represents a particularly expensive kind of transaction per unit of distance so that any given set of employment places—if they are to be viable—must always co-exist in close spatial association with a set of workers' residential locations.

Three main analytical points flow from this observation. First, whenever employment places and workers' residences converge spatially, processes of job search, recruitment, and matching are facilitated because any given quantum of labor-market information can be circulated that much more easily among the relevant parties. Second, by dint of shared patterns of habituation, the work-force as a whole will come to be imbued with skills and aptitudes attuned to agglomeration-specific needs. Third, with the assemblage of a large work-force in one place, it becomes feasible to provide multifaceted educational and training programs responsive to the requirements of the local production system.

All of these local labor-market features are strongly interlaced with increasing-returns effects so that the larger the agglomeration, the more efficient its operation will tend to be. In the same way, the *per capita* costs of providing infrastructural artifacts and other public goods with high fixed costs and productivity-boosting virtues (such as expressways, airports, street-cleaning services, and so on) will usually be lower in large agglomerations than in small.

---

[17] For a full discussion of the issues involved here, see J. Peck, *Work-Place: The Social Regulation of Labor Markets*, New York: Guilford, 1996; see also A. J. Scott, *Metropolis: From the Division of Labor to Urban Form*, Berkeley and Los Angeles: University of California Press, 1988.

One final major point about the transactional foundations of agglomeration needs to be made. Transactions are a crucial element of those beneficial 'atmospheric' effects that are indispensable if production complexes are to emerge not just as amalgams of capital and labor, but also as communities and as systems of untraded interdependencies; and again, their efficacy is enhanced by mutual proximity of the various participants. Proximity makes possible frequent personalized encounters between many different individuals occupying many different kinds of socio-economic niches, and thus positively encourages the evolution of distinctive local cultures. These cultures facilitate economically useful processes of socialization, and they provide an important context of mutual understandings within which learning and innovation can proceed at an accelerated rate (though they can also sometimes be a hindrance to development by placing barriers in the way of advantageous change). Learning and innovation are further enhanced by the constant interchanges of information that occur in industrial agglomerations.[18] The general idea is felicitously captured in the following account of traditional waggon-building in rural England at the turn of the century, an account in which the socialized nature of the knowledge base of the craft is clearly expressed:

The lore was a tangled network of country prejudices, whose reasons were known in some respects here, in others there, and so on. In farm-yard, in tap-room, at market, the details were discussed over and over again; they were gathered together for remembrance in village workshops; carters, smiths, farmers, wheelmakers, in thousands handed on each his own little bit of understanding, passing it to his son or to the wheel-wright of the day, linking up the centuries. But for the most part, the details were but dimly understood; the whole body of knowledge was a mystery, a piece of folk-knowledge residing in the folk collectively but never wholly in any individual.[19]

Despite the reference to country prejudices, the same essential processes of social exchange and information circulation are critical to the operation of modern industrial regions, even such high-technology industrial regions as Orange County, California, with its advanced electronics manufacturers, or San Diego, with its burgeoning biotechnology industry. Regions where this sort of interchange occurs on a major scale are often hotbeds of creativity, as illustrated by the streams

[18] R. Florida, 'Toward the learning region', *Futures*, 27 (1995): 527–36.
[19] G. Sturt, *The Wheelwright's Shop*, Cambridge: Cambridge University Press, 1923, p. 74.

of technological innovations that characterized the cotton textile industry in nineteenth-century Lancashire, or that are discernible in the semiconductor industry in Silicon Valley today. This endemic creativity of at least some agglomerations often endows them with absolute competitive advantages in production, enabling them to command global markets so long as they stay at the forefront of innovation.

Even in a purely static world, then, agglomeration is a forceful mechanism for begetting and appropriating many economic and social benefits. The dynamic aspects of agglomerations greatly magnify these properties.

The dynamic theory

Romer has shown that situations where increasing returns effects prevail are characterized by a temporal logic in which growth leads constantly onward to yet more growth.[20] Concomitantly, in any given regional cluster at any given instant, we are unlikely to detect anything even approaching static equilibrium. What we are much more sure to observe is a cross-section through a developmental trajectory that can be understood only in terms of a path-dependent process of evolution and adjustment structured by the phenomenon of agglomeration economies.[21]

At the outset, we need to relate the preceding remarks to a basic description of growth and change in articulated economic spaces and derivative agglomerations. I have already indicated that quantitative increases in the market demand for any particular product often lead to the formation of new and specialized tasks or trades in production systems, and these will constitute independent sectors if vertical disintegration also comes about. The process is accentuated where we have flexible production systems facing much uncertainty and instability so that frequent adjustments of process and product configurations occur, as in the case of heavily urbanized sectors like high-technology electronics, craft manufacturing (e.g. clothing), cultural-products industries, or business services. Thus, as markets expand, we often observe a corresponding pattern of industrial change as

[20] P. M. Romer, 'Increasing returns and long-run growth', *Journal of Political Economy*, 94 (1986): 1002–37.

[21] Cf. N. Kaldor, 'The case for regional policies', *Scottish Journal of Political Economy*, 17 (1970): 337–47; R. R. Nelson and S. G. Winter, *An Evolutionary Theory of Economic Change*, Cambridge, Mass.: Belknap Press, 1982.

depicted in Figure 5.3. What is shown here in very schematic outline is an industrial complex undergoing transformation both in the horizontal dimension (i.e. increases in the number of production establishments of any given type) and in the vertical dimension (i.e. increases in the number of different sectors as a result of dynamic vertical disintegration). To be sure, this pattern of change can always be undercut at any time by technological innovations that provoke radical resyntheses of the social division of labor, but so long as it continues it will exhibit the processes of division, diversification, multiplication, and specialization as described. For the sake of argument, I shall assume that the complex depicted in Figure 5.3 is endowed with strong static agglomeration economies at all times throughout its evolution.

I shall further take it for granted that this complex, as it begins to make its appearance on the economic landscape, is indifferent to existing macro-geographic arrangements, and that it is viable—initially at least—in a wide variety of locations. Hence, this imaginary complex in its infant stage is not too dissimilar from a number of familiar empirical cases, such as cars in the 1890s, aircraft assembly in the early decades of the present century, or semiconductors in the 1950s. This means that the locational structure of the infant industry will be largely indeterminate from an economic point of view. Its early geography can be seen simply as an 'accident'—an effect, for example, of where its founding figure(s) happened to be living, or a result of a peculiar constellation of political forces in a particular place at a particular time.

Let us suppose for the sake of argument that this structure comprises several different locales, no one of which has any special pregiven advantage over the others. Even so, small chance events alone are likely to push one locale into a leading position, if only in the sense that it begins to expand more rapidly than the others.[22] In other instances, a given locale may experience in the post-infant industry stage what we might designate as a 'breakthrough moment', namely, a decisive commercial or technological incident that pushes it to the forefront of development. Examples of this phenomenon are Henry Ford's organizational and managerial experiments in Detroit, Donald Douglas's development of the DC-3 aircraft in Los Angeles, and, arguably, the establishment of the Fairchild Semiconductor plant (with its internal managerial dysfunctions and subsequent spin-offs) in

[22] W. B. Arthur, 'Silicon Valley locational clusters: when do increasing returns imply monopoly?' *Mathematical Social Sciences*, 19 (1990), 235–51.

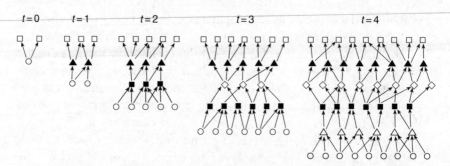

FIG. 5.3. A growing industrial complex with dynamic vertical disintegration, showing evolution of the system from three establishments in two sectors at $t = 0$ to forty-seven establishments in six sectors at $t = 4$

Silicon Valley. Once this occurs, there is a good chance that the locale will start to consolidate and extend its lead, especially where increasing returns and dynamic learning effects come into play. Because of lock-in effects, an early start is in fact often critical to long-run success in these kinds of system.

Provided that markets continue to grow, the leading locale is now likely to be subject to a many-sided process of developmental self-transformation in which the agglomeration processes described earlier will be greatly amplified. There is apt to be further elaboration of the social division of labor leading to economic diversification and increased economic synergies over a limited area. Concomitantly, local labor markets will grow, and new labor skills will almost certainly emerge. The industrial atmosphere of the locale will tend to become more finely delineated, and the business community may well begin to acquire identifiable cultural attributes marked by distinctive conventions and routines. Information exchanges and learning effects will become increasingly densely textured, with a corresponding sharpening of the stimuli to innovation. The ramifying social division of labor will in turn throw out more and more commercial opportunities, thus stimulating new entrepreneurial efforts. As these processes move forward, a complex regional economic system will progressively consolidate its geographic presence, and—at least for a time—will evolve forward on the basis of its deepening stock of external economies of scale and scope.

There are always, of course, numerous hazards (including the onset of agglomeration diseconomies) scattered along this pathway of development, and things do not always work out in practice quite so unproblematically, as illustrated by the cases of regional collapse that occur from time to time. However, once a region has made a good head start, so that increasing returns are being generated with some intensity and its competitive advantages are being continually sharpened, it will tend over some fairly long-run period to follow a recursive growth trajectory, providing that markets for its outputs remain healthy. This kind of growth is typically associated with lock-in, in the sense that many indurated and mutually reinforcing relationships within the regional economy will ensure that its trajectory acquires a marked dependence on its past.[23] This does not signify that the region

---

[23] P. A. David, 'Clio and the economics of QWERTY', *American Economic Review*, 75 (1985), 332–7.

will now be set irrevocably on a course to one final historical desti-
nation. To the contrary, even though lock-in implies that the region's
development is path-dependent, it is also consistent with the existence of many branching-points representing conjunctures where the
regional economy may move in any one of a number of different possible directions. Once it has moved, however, its future is then to that
degree committed.

Unless there are bounds to the continued appropriation of increasing returns effects by producers in the region, development will continue in this manner, and there is some likelihood that sooner or later
the region will become a pioneering center of development in its specialized domain of economic activity. Thus, what began as a footloose
infant industry, will now—in this ideal-typical world—have attained
a stage of geographical and historical development where it can be
effectively carried on only in a limited number of locational contexts,
i.e. those that provide just the right kinds of agglomeration economies
and competitive advantages. By the same token, regions that fail to
make an early start in fostering the development of a particular industry, or that fall behind in some way, are susceptible to 'lock-out' in
the sense that they are liable to find it increasingly difficult to catch
up with—much less overtake—the leading contenders.

A HISTORICAL GEOGRAPHIC PERSPECTIVE

A differentiated system of production agglomerations has always been
an essential feature of capitalism, and in one way or another these
agglomerations can generally be understood in terms of the abstracted
principles outlined above. In practice, however, these principles always
operate in unique geographical and historical contexts, resulting in
very different kinds of contingent effects from case to case. Also, and
quite apart from the repercussions that variables such as sector, scale
of production, market conditions, or nation may have on the way these
principles function, they are always subject to massive recomposition by reason of periodic shifts in the modalities of accumulation in
capitalism.

Three brief examples may be advanced to illustrate the importance
of the interplay between the systematic and the contingent in mold-
ing actual patterns of regional development at distinctively different
periods of economic history. Equally, they serve to re-emphasize the
idea of the present conjuncture of historical geography as a nexus of

socio-economic relationships that will itself in due course be subject to fundamental restructuring.

The first example refers to the workshop and factory system that came so strongly to the fore in Britain in the first half of the nineteenth century, and that gave rise to a veritable revolution in patterns of regional development at that time. Major segments of the industrial apparatus in early nineteenth-century Britain were made up of small and vertically disintegrated firms at the core of dense transactional networks. The geography of production was accordingly, and to a major extent, arranged in classical Marshallian industrial districts forming much of the economic base of the manufacturing towns that characterized the period. Familiar examples are cottons in Lancashire, woollens in Yorkshire, cutlery in Sheffield, and the various metal trades of Birmingham. An impoverished urban working class keeping these industries going was constantly replenished by a massive drift of population from the countryside to the city—a contingent but critical condition of survival for the entire system.

Another example is offered by the system of fordist mass production that flourished in the United States from the 1920s to the 1960s, and which also brought about significant transformations of the economic landscape. In this instance, and to reiterate some of the information already presented in Chapter 2, the leading edges of production were to a great degree embodied in the lead plants of growth pole industries around which multi-tiered complexes of suppliers congealed in both functional and spatial terms. Such complexes typically constituted the foundations of the overgrown industrial metropolitan regions of the twentieth century. They were also the fountainhead of the blue-collar/white-collar social structures that characterized the cities of the US Manufacturing Belt over this period, and that were then re-expressed in distinctive patterns of socially segmented neighborhood development.[24] By the end of the 1970s, the competitive energies of fordist mass production were all but exhausted in most of the advanced capitalist countries, leading to a severe and prolonged crisis of the metropolitan areas that had grown up in response to its developmental thrust over the previous half-century.

A third and last example is presented by contemporary processes of post-fordist industrialization. This third case is distinguished by a

---

[24] The classical account of this phenomenon can be found in R. E. Park, E. W. Burgess, and R. D. McKenzie, *The City*, Chicago: Chicago University Press, 1925.

multiplicity of flexible production networks in industries as diverse as fashion clothing, furniture, electronic components, biotechnology, films, and financial services, and concomitantly by a resurgence of industrial districts and agglomerations across the globe, even in areas located in what was formerly widely viewed as a development-resistant periphery. In their turn, the regions that have most actively participated in this type of industrialization now also find themselves bound tightly together in world-wide webs of interdependence, with multinational firms playing a major role in mediating between the local and the global. As a corollary, and in contrast to the older centralized multinationals of High Fordism, these newer global firms are often quite fragmented in terms of their command structure and functional organization. The privileged foci of this curent model of industrialization and urban development are the big regional motors of the new global economy, especially in North America, Western Europe, and East and South-east Asia.

This latest episode in the historical geography of capitalism is based on production systems that tend to be quite fragmented and diversified, and yet which are also capable of efficient operation at many different levels of scale, individually or collectively.[25] We might say —very schematically—that, whereas nineteenth-century workshop and factory systems were able to produce variety of output but were limited in the total scale that they could achieve, and whereas fordist mass production freed industry from quantitative restraint but at the expense of product variety, modern flexible production systems (with the aid of new electronic and information technologies) are able to achieve considerable variety of output while they can also often attain significant scale effects. Further, because post-fordist, flexible production systems are generally strongly externalized and transactions-intensive, regional agglomeration seems to be again resurgent, in contrast with the steady break-up of many industrial regions that was occurring as fordism approached its climacteric. Regions are once more emerging as foci of production and repositories of specialized know-how and technological capability, even as the globalization of economic relationships proceeds at an accelerating rate.

[25] M. J. Piore and C. F. Sabel, *The Second Industrial Divide: Possibilities for Prosperity*, New York: Basic Books, 1984; B. Coriat, *L'Atelier et le Robot*, Paris: Christian Bourgois, 1990.

6

Collective Order and Regional Development: Social and Cultural Regulation of Local Economic Systems

THE REGULATORY IMPERATIVE

One of the most powerful and practically influential ideas in twentieth-century social science is represented by the general equilibrium market model of neoclassical economics. This model purports to demonstrate, among other things, that when competition is perfectly decentralized and atomized economic systems will attain to a perfect harmony between all demands, supplies, and prices such that maximal allocative efficiency will be secured. The model, in addition, constitutes the foundation for much of what currently passes for ordinary common sense about how modern capitalism functions, or at least how it *ought* to function if only certain irrational structural impediments to its full concrete realization (foremost among them being government bureaucracies) could be swept away.

Ordinary common sense, of course, is always open to question and reformulation, even when it is based on what appears to be a sophisticated rationale. Let me insist at the outset that this remark is not a prelude to an attempted denial of the virtues of competition and markets in the ordering of economic life. On the contrary, the allocative efficiency that competition and markets promote is a most desirable objective, and a crucial condition of long-run economic growth and prosperity. However, two major qualifying statements must be immediately advanced. One is that competition and markets are not free-floating social phenomena; rather, and as already intimated in previous chapters, they are shaped and made possible by an underlying framework of institutions and conventions (e.g. patterns of property ownership, modes of corporate organization, managerial practices and ideologies, the legal system, norms of socialization).[1] The other is that

---

[1] K. Polanyi, *The Great Transformation: The Political and Economic Origins of Our Times*, New York: Rinehart, 1944.

competition and markets do not operate unproblematically, but have a pervasive tendency—in empirical reality—to fail to work in the efficient manner predicted by the neoclassical model. A *laisser-faire* economic order in the full and final sense of the term can exist only in libertarian fantasies, for capitalism is congenitally incapable of reproducing the mainsprings of its own internal logic without the aid of extra-capitalist social infrastructures. This is not just because pure *laisser-faire* economic activity is susceptible to technical conditions of market failure (such as the free-rider problem, or the fact that information is not, as the model assumes, a universally available free good); nor is it because the market often yields outcomes that run counter to pre-defined social goals (such as the maintenance of a minimum standard of living for workers, or the protection of cultural values that are threatened by commercial interests)—though all of these vitiating circumstances are sufficiently serious in and of themselves. Even more important for the present discussion is the circumstance that superior levels of long-run economic efficiency and performance are almost always attainable where certain forms of collective order and action are brought into play *in combination with* competition and markets.[2]

The latter proposition, of course, does not signify that any collective intrusion into the economy is always preferable to no intrusion at all. What it does purport to say is that there is a legitimate domain of inquiry focused on what precise substantive forms of collective intervention, in combination with individual market-based decision-making and action, will secure stability combined with outstanding economic performance in any given set of empirical circumstances; and it implies, concomitantly, that there is also a legitimate domain of social and political practices focused on how exactly to bring the requisite balance between collective and the individual order into empirical effect.

Regulationist theory, as introduced in Chapter 1, has begun the task of dealing with problems such as these, but mainly in terms of non-spatial macro-economic issues. Regulationists have looked especially at how institutions of economic governance take shape, both

---

[2] A. H. Amsden, *Asia's Next Giant: South Korea and Late Industrialization*, New York: Oxford University Press, 1992; R. Wade, *Governing the Market: Economic Theory and the Role of Government in East Asian Industrialization*, Princeton: Princeton University Press, 1990.

spontaneously and voluntaristically, in relation to specific dysfunctions at different historical moments in: (*a*) technology systems, (*b*) production complexes and labor relations, (*c*) the distribution of income across various social groups and classes, and (*d*) aggregate demand.[3] But there is clearly a pressing need also to examine governance issues in a regional context, and to inquire into the developmental potentialities of specifically regional forms of economic regulation. This need stems not only from the inherent instability of competitive market economies, but also from the observation that regional economic systems possess vital collective properties that evade private ownership, but have decisive impacts on the economic prospects and livelihood of all individual firms and workers within their purview. It follows at once that these collective properties are rightfully objectives of public policy and social choice.

In point of fact, there is now a growing volume of theoretical ideas and practical experiences concerned precisely with the question of regional economic governance, which can be characterized in general as an emerging corpus of neo-Listian approaches to understanding and building local competitive advantage. This work is posited largely on the notion that the most effective way of fostering beneficial externalities involves institution-building from the bottom up rather than indicative planning from the top down, and it focuses more than anything else on those specifically place-bound webs of economic relationships that are the quintessential feature of agglomeration as such.[4] It involves two intersecting types of collective decision-making and behavior. One is concerned with intensifying the spontaneous social and cultural bases of civic atmosphere (e.g. by working toward more collaborative forms of business activity); the other is more concerned with setting up formal organizational infrastructures in pursuit of regional economic advantage (e.g. by establishing technology diffusion centers or labor-training institutions). Moreover, these kinds of activity are not necessarily the monopoly of governmental agencies in the usually accepted sense of the term, but also may occur within

[3] R. Boyer and Y. Saillard (eds.), *Théorie de la Régulation: l'Etat de Savoirs*, Paris: La Découverte, 1995.

[4] See e.g. D. Leborgne and A. Lipietz, 'Conceptual fallacies and open questions on post-fordism', in M. Storper and A. J. Scott (eds.) *Pathways to Industrialization and Regional Development*, London: Routledge, 1992, pp. 332–48; M. Storper and A. J. Scott, 'The wealth of regions: market forces and policy imperatives in local and global context', *Futures*, 27 (1995): 505–26.

purely civil and quasi-civil organizations such as manufacturers' guilds, labor syndicates, not-for-profit associations, *kanban* circles, joint ventures, private–public partnerships, and so on. Indeed, institutions like these have spread rapidly at all geographical scales in the modern world, posing urgent and puzzling questions about the directions of historical change in patterns of economic governance at regional, national, plurinational, and global levels.

A BACKWARD GLANCE

The new varieties of regional collective action and strategic choice that we see emerging today contrast markedly with more traditional versions of regional planning which, in their heyday at least, tended to be less concerned with all-out growth than with redistributive programs of various sorts.

Regional planning, in its modern guise, made its historical appearance in the 1930s in the aftermath of the Great Depression, as one of the instruments of the dawning keynesian welfare-statist policy system. From the first, it owed its ascendance to central government initiatives in North America and Western Europe, and it consisted primarily of efforts to assist regions that had been adversely affected by the Depression and were faced with problems of chronic structural unemployment. Among these regions were Appalachia in the United States and the older coalfield areas of northern England and central Scotland.

It was only after the Second World War, however, and especially in the 1950s and 1960s, that regional planning came into its own as a really major adjunct to keynesian welfare-statist regulation. Above all, it now became pre-eminently a set of procedures for re-equilibrating national spaces by means of the redistribution of resources from prosperous core regions to failing or stagnant peripheral regions. Throughout North America and Western Europe, new governmental bodies were set up with the objective of reducing regional disparities, a goal that they sought to achieve through measures to stimulate growth in lagging peripheral regions via financial subsidies, infrastructure provision, job training schemes, industrialization programs, and so on. Representative of such bodies were the Economic Development Administration in the United States, the Department of Regional Economic Expansion in Canada, the Department of Economic Affairs in Britain, the Délégation à l'Aménagement du Territoire in France, and the Cassa per il Mezzogiorno in Italy. In some parts of the periphery (e.g.

southern Italy or Fos-sur-Mer in France) efforts were also made to create important new growth centers through lavish investment in physical infrastructure and the offer of major financial incentives to plants in growth-pole industries to locate nearby. Most of these initiatives, unfortunately, failed to create the sort of endogenous dynamisms necessary for sustained regional growth, and all the more so because they were more often than not focused on industries that had entered the mature post-entrepreneurial phase of the product cycle.[5]

Regionally based growth-pole policies were tried, too, in a number of less developed countries such as Brazil, Mexico, and Malaysia, where in the 1960s and 1970s they were rather over-ambitiously seen as an avenue to accelerated national economic growth.[6] Such policies were usually combined with import substitution, for a two-pronged strategy that linked growth-pole development with progressive industrialization in upstream sectors was thought of as a particularly effective and realizable method of stimulating growth. Again, however, the results were mixed at best, partly because domestic limitations on aggregate demand undercut the possibility of achieving requisite economies of scale, and partly because growth-pole development was so dependent on Western capital and technology that it greatly accentuated the severe debt crisis of many Third World countries in the 1970s.

Meanwhile, with the unravelling of fordist mass production and its keynesian welfare-statist underpinnings over the 1970s, associated structures of redistributive regional planning also started to crumble throughout the developed economies. In many of these economies, regional per capita income convergence,[7] together with the foward surge of many important new industrial spaces in what were formerly peripheral areas, meant that the regional question at that time was no longer so urgently concentrated on issues of disparity or backwardness as it previously was. In the new economic environment of the 1970s and 1980s, the principal question now was rather how to maintain prosperity *tout court*, and this in turn became reflected in a series of steady long-term reductions in economically unproductive public expenses.

[5] Cf. H. B. Chenery, 'Development policies for Southern Italy', *Quarterly Journal of Economics*, 76 (1962): 515–48.

[6] N. Hansen, B. Higgins, and D. J. Savoie, *Regional Policy in a Changing World*, New York: Plenum Press, 1990.

[7] Cf. R. J. Barro and X. Sala-i-Martin, 'Convergence across states and regions', Economic Growth Center Discussion Paper no. 629, Yale University, 1991.

Even the most successful regions, however, were starting to evince signs of severe economic stress, and many were caught in a powerful pincer movement which heightened the pressure. On the one hand, the rising tide of competition due to globalization, and especially the intensified export activities of Japan and the newly industrializing countries, was undercutting traditional industries in virtually all parts of North America and Western Europe. On the other hand, the shift in the political climate toward neo-conservatism, as marked first of all by thatcherism in Britain and reaganism in the United States but then spreading rapidly to other industrialized countries, meant that national governments were increasingly reluctant to interpose themselves between the global forces exerting this strain and the individual regions where its effects appeared on the ground in a wide range of localized effects. As a consequence, over the 1980s and especially the 1990s, many regions started to engage in various experimental exercises in alternative forms of local institution-building and self-help in order to preserve their economic well-being and future prospects.[8]

The latter trend has been further encouraged by the fact that, as post-fordist economic restructuring took deeper and deeper hold after the late 1970s, many new kinds of regional production systems began to spring forth, often with peculiar configurations of actual and latent collective order. Among the important shifts occasioned by this restructuring were pervasive substitutions of flexible externalized value-added networks for fordist-style internalized vertical hierarchies, and of more volatile, competitive labor markets for the relatively stable employment system of fordism. Regions where such changes were occurring with special intensity were as a result faced with rising predicaments rooted in the increasing externalization and destabilization of economic relationships combined with many new possibilities for reaping agglomeration economies by means of coordinated action. They were, and are, thus confronted with policy challenges emanating both from the new competitive climate in which they have found themselves and from the new operating logics that govern their internal economic order.

---

[8] A. M. Isserman, 'State economic development policy and practice in the United States: a survey article', *International Regional Science Review*, 16 (1994): 49–100; J. Schmandt and R. Wilson (eds.), *Promoting High-Technology Industry: Initiatives and Policies for State Governments*, Boulder, Colo.: Westview, 1987.

SOCIO-CULTURAL REGULATION AND REGIONAL STRATEGIC CHOICE

On the basis of the earlier discussion, I take it that these policy challenges should focus above all on eliciting maximum regional externalities in order to promote local competitive advantage while at the same time ensuring that socially agreed-upon standards of communal well-being are preserved. The social and political tools for the pursuit of these goals can be described succinctly in terms of both an informal set of mechanisms that sustain economically useful regional cultures and conventions, and a formal set of institutions and organizations that help to magnify local reserves of agglomeration economies.

Informal structures of local regulation

When Marshall advanced the notion of atmosphere, he had explicitly in mind all those aspects of tradition and social life that impinge positively on the economic performance of particular places.[9] In Marshall's original account, these phenomena were seen as being entirely spontaneous and unplanned, and so they were (and remain) to a large degree. That said, a comprehension of their origins and dynamics can also help us think about the possibilities of devising more self-conscious ways of promoting their positive effects. At the risk of some repetition of information already presented in the previous chapter, let us look again at the complex role of culture as a collective attribute of regional economic systems. Three points may be briefly advanced here.

First, regional cultures not only facilitate the socialization of individuals in various ways, but also are bearers of significant informal knowledge effects. Because of these effects, most regions—even those that are centers of advanced high-technology industry—operate as important repositories of tacit know-how that is not codified or centralized in any formal manner.[10] Certain varieties of civil association

[9] A remarkable and much-overlooked early contribution along similar lines can be found in E. E. Lampard, 'The history of cities in economically advanced areas', *Economic Development and Cultural Change*, 3 (1955): 81–102.

[10] M. Castells and P. Hall, *Technopoles of the World: The Making of 21st Century Industrial Complexes*, London: Routledge, 1994.

can greatly sharpen the functional capacities of regions in this regard. For example, some types of guild, or producers' organization, or trade alliance can provide the instruments of social contact and the normative frameworks that will enhance smooth socio-economic integration and mutually beneficial exchanges of information.

Second, and concomitantly, regional agglomerations of producers are almost always sites of accumulated cultural conventions, social rituals, and routinized forms of personal interchange that help to guide behavior into appropriate channels and allow individuals to make reasoned assessments about the expected performance of other individuals in different business situations. Reputation effects are an element of this process, and they are of special importance in cases (the financial services sector of the City of London, for example) where markets are volatile and quick action is often essential.[11] Cut-throat competition and the endemic distrust that is bred by economic individualism are liable to dissolve away the subtle social threads by which such systems of collective effects are usually held together, and some self-conscious type of intervention is often needed to provide the fiduciary guarantees that make possible the effective sharing of resources, skills, and know-how in the interests of improved regional competitive advantage. Many analysts of late have suggested that the success of industrial communities in places like Japan and the Third Italy is built in large measure upon just such trust-based relationships as these, together with the underlying forms of social organization (from the *keiretsu*-style associations in the former to frequent consultation and concertation of action between local government, management, and unions in the latter) that foster them.[12]

[11] M. Pryke, 'An international city going global: spatial change in the City of London', *Environment and Planning D: Society and Space*, 9 (1991): 197–222; N. Thrift, 'On the social and cultural determinants of international financial centers: the case of the City of London', in S. Corbridge, R. Martin and N. Thrift (eds.), *Money, Power and Space*, Oxford: Blackwell, 1994, pp. 327–55.

[12] G. Becattini, 'The Marshallian industrial district as a socio-economic notion', in F. Pyke, G. Becattini, and W. Sengenberger (eds.), *Industrial Districts and Intra-Firm Cooperation in Italy*, Geneva: International Institute for Labour Studies, 1990, pp. 37–74; D. B. Friedman, *The Misunderstood Miracle: Industrial Development and Political Change in Japan*, Ithaca, NY: Cornell University Press, 1988; E. H. Lorenz, 'Trust, community, and cooperation: toward a theory of industrial districts', in M. Storper and A. J. Scott (eds.), *Pathways to Industrialization and Regional Development*, London: Routledge, 1992, pp. 195–204; R. D. Putnam, *Making Democracy Work: Civic Traditions in Modern Italy*, Princeton: Princeton University Press, 1993.

Third, the commercial products of some regions often have an identifiable cachet in the sense that they possess a unique look, feel, and semiotic content which in turn is based on cultural assets embedded in local production networks, local labor markets, and the general local environment. This phenomenon is particularly evident in the case of design-intensive outputs from the craft, fashion, and cultural-products industries generally. For example, the film industry of Los Angeles—or more narrowly of Hollywood—draws on an elaborate web of local cultural references and sensitivities (much of them embodied in the skills of directors, actors, writers, musicians, make-up artists, camera operators, lighting technicians, etc.). As a result, the film industry is able to produce streams of products that not only are technically accomplished, but also have unique and indeed inimitable emanations that appeal to vast numbers of consumers. The same products in their turn create images (real or imagined) of Los Angeles/Hollywood that are then assimilated back into the city's fund of cultural assets where they become available as inputs to new rounds of production.

One consequence of these relationships is that the reputation and authenticity of cultural and quasi-cultural products (qualities that often provide decisive competitive advantages in trade) are sometimes irrevocably tied to particular places—think of Danish furniture, Florentine leather goods, Parisian *haute couture*, Champagne wines, London theater, Swiss watches before digitization, Thai silks, recorded music from Nashville, or, again, Hollywood films. Collective action is frequently essential to sustain the cultural-*cum*-economic virtues of such places and to safeguard their products and reputations from the negative influence of cheap imitations.

In sum, local cultures often provide a many-sided boost to processes of regional economic development and growth, and there is much that can be done in terms of social and political action to ensure their continued viability. Amin and Thrift have shown how such regional cultures and their sustaining social infrastructures operate in the specific cases of the craft industries of Italy and the financial services industry of the City of London, and they have gone on to claim that 'institutional thickness' is one of their indispensable qualities.[13]

---

[13] A. Amin and N. Thrift, 'Neo-marshallian nodes in global networks', *International Journal of Urban and Regional Research*, 16 (1992): 571–87.

The problem with this formulation, however, is that, while sustaining infrastructures are certainly essential for the maintenance of local atmosphere, and thickness may sometimes be an advantage, not all forms of institutional thickness provide an automatic guarantee of economic dynamism. Indeed, institutional thickness can be a positive hindrance to development and growth where stubbornly dysfunctional attitudes and habits are firmly locked in to the local economic system. There are numerous empirical cases of stagnant or declining industrial districts in which individual producers have strong and durable trust relationships with one another, but are nonetheless unable to turn the tide of their dwindling collective fortunes.

The point is well exemplified by the case of the Los Angeles jewelry industry, where trust is extremely well developed (as it must be in such a business if transactions are to be carried out with reasonable dispatch), but where the industry is by and large enmeshed in a system of short-sighted cost-cutting behaviors and unimaginative product designs that greatly impede its ability to break out of its status as a lethargic, second-rate center of production.[14] This state of affairs may be contrasted with the current condition of the jewelry industry of Bangkok, Thailand, which, despite its less highly developed trust environment, has been able to outperform the Los Angeles industry by far. Producers in Bangkok have built up a remarkable political capacity to mobilize all segments of the industry around common goals and objectives (such as the establishment of gem-cutting and jewelry-design training centers), and to pressure government for favorable legislation. In contrast to mere institutional thickness, it is the disciplined and focused forms of political mobilization of the Thai jewelry industry and its representatives that have enabled it to become one of the major jewelry producers and exporters in the modern world.

Consider, too, the case of the Hollywood film industry, where a fast-moving game of collaborative ventures, but of intermittent defection and betrayal too, creates a situation in which trust can never become conventionalized or ossified. One of the consequences of this is a high degree of relational fluidity in the industry, but also a continual evasion of the dangers of stasis.

[14] A. J. Scott, 'Variations on the theme of agglomeration and growth: the gem and jewelry industry in Los Angeles and Bangkok', *Geoforum*, 25 (1994): 249–63.

Formal structures of local regulation

We can observe in many regional economic systems today not only dense overlays of informal coordinating mechanisms, but also much formal social regulation, both governmental and civil.

A large part of this formal regulation, of course, is comprised of familiar types of urban- and regional-planning activity in the domains of transportation, land use, housing, and so on. To an ever-increasing degree, however, these familiar (though also critically necessary) types of planning are being complemented by an altogether different species of local public action whose objectives are focused more on promoting such effects as entrepreneurship, technological excellence, useful labor skills, and regional competitive advantage generally. There are many cases where action of this sort has been remarkably successful, especially where it has concentrated on the provision of institutional services that add significantly to total agglomeration economies. Five main generic categories of such action can be distinguished. All can be observed in various institutional configurations in advanced regions throughout much of the developed world today.

Provision of new technology and design services   In spite of patents and other instruments of business protection, it is difficult for firms to internalize all of the economic benefits that flow from their investments in new technological knowledge. The persistent leakiness of this knowledge leads to serious market-failure problems in that firms endemically under-invest in necessary research, particularly if they are small in size and have only limited financial resources. Market failure is also a feature of design innovations that can be easily copied and debased by competitors so that the initial private investment in creating any design is rapidly devalorized. However, technological research and design services can often be efficiently organized on a socialized or collective basis, especially in regional contexts where the local economy is highly specialized, and where there are thus likely to be significant overall economies of scale that accrue to any public effort.

Various kinds of publicly funded centers offering these services have been proliferating in regions throughout North America, Western Europe, and Japan over the last couple of decades. One specific example is offered by the government-sponsored network of Centres Régionaux d'Innovation et de Transfert de Technologie that has been set up across France with each center providing specialized information and advice (e.g. in biotechnology, microelectronics, robotics, and so) depending on local needs. Similarly, the Steinbeis Foundation, a private non-profit organization, has been extremely effective in Baden-Württemberg in local technology-transfer activities.[15]

Worker education and training   Here too severe market failures are common, for any investments that private firms make in upgrading the quality of their labor force are apt to be dissipated or appropriated by competitors when workers shift jobs. This problem is rendered more acute in regional economic systems where firms share jointly in common labor pools. General provision of instructional services for workers is therefore essential if long-run economic viability is to be maintained, and it is likely to be particularly effective where agglomeration-specific skills and aptitudes are in strong demand. Accordingly, one of the most familiar types of collective activity to be found in econo-mically growing regions at the present time is concerned with worker training. Labor unions, trade associations, municipal governments, and other public agencies are all heavily engaged in this sort of activity. Colleges and universities, too, are an important element of the fabric of regional training institutions, and they often gear their curricula to the needs and orientations of local production complexes. This trend appears to be very much on the increase at the present time.

Collaborative networks   Dense regional economies can usually be decomposed into underlying systems of value-added networks. These networks offer important opportunities for institution-building to sup-port collaborative interactions and to ensure that all resources held by individual firms in any network are fully deployed. A notable advant-age of collaboration is that firms can then specialize in core compe-tencies while retaining some measure of confidence in the durability and consistency of their relations with suppliers and purchasers. Japanese producers have been particularly successful in organizing themselves into collaborative networks together with appropriate sys-tems of governance. Such networks encourage high levels of inter-dependence among all participants, ranging from the finely tuned

---

[15] P. Cooke and K. Morgan, 'The regional innovation system in Baden-Württemberg', *International Journal of Technology Management*, 9 (1994): 394–429.

just-in-time transmission of inputs and outputs throughout their entire extent, to technology sharing and mutual financial aid.

Regional marketing services   Successful pursuit of high-performance production and commercialization of goods and services hinges on the ability to penetrate, sustain, and shape consumer market niches. Yet the mass of small firms that typically constitute the main elements of any regional economic system rarely have the resources individually to engage in the information-gathering, market development, and advertising activities necessary for such pursuits. Local governments and industry associations in many of the more successful industrial districts in the 'Third Italy' (north-east and central Italy) and elsewhere have been notably adept in providing collective marketing services through advertising local products, organizing trade shows and fairs, providing critical information on export opportunities, and so on. Formalized procedures for trademarking and labeling, thus providing guarantees of product quality and authenticity, can also be extremely helpful to local firms in maintaining existing markets and opening up new outlets. For example, Furniture New York is a successful consortium of some thirty-three designers and furniture manufacturers that has been operating since 1990 with the aid of funding from the New York State Department of Economic Development, and it now engages in globally recognized branding of all participants' products.[16]

Other services   A rapid scan of the recent literature on industrial districts and regional development instantly brings to light a wide variety of miscellaneous service organizations operating in a bewildering variety of public and private institutional formats. They range from community banking and investment facilities for small firms, through agencies that supply what Brusco has called 'real services' such as accounting and payroll preparation,[17] to private/public organizations like Joint Venture Silicon Valley or the Bay Area Multimedia Partnership, offering complex coordinating services for a large and multifaceted local constituency.

[16] D. Brown, 'Furniture New York: taking more than ideas from Northern Italy', *Firm Connections*, 2/3 (1994): 3 and 8.

[17] S. Brusco, 'Small firms and the provision of real services', in F. Pyke and W. Sengenberger (eds.), *Industrial Districts and Local Economic Regeneration*, Geneva: International Institute of Labour Studies, 1992, pp. 176–92.

In these and other ways, the developed post-fordist regions of the contemporary world are now engaging in an extraordinarily diverse series of initiatives and experiments as they seek to discover the most practically useful bases for the collective contestation of markets in the new global competition.[18] Simultaneously, we are beginning to observe not just the emergence of new varieties of regional economic order, but also the formation of radically new kinds of regional political initiative.

Temporal steering of regional economies

These informal and formal structures of local economic regulation take on added significance in the context of dynamic processes of regional development. Not only are they the essential building-blocks of static regional competitive advantage, but they also provide many of the conditions under which a rising flow of agglomeration economies is secured over time. However, in view of the path dependency, branching, and temporal lock-in characteristics of local economies, real problems of dynamic strategic choice and coordination are apt to pose themselves. Above all, some form of overall ability to steer the regional economy is crucial, because options that seem to be unattractive in the near future may sometimes evolve into very desirable development trajectories over the long run, while attractive near-term options can lock in to significantly inferior sets of outcomes with the passage of time. Coordinated mechanisms of regional strategic choice provide an important capacity for guiding the regional economy around problematical corners of the branching process.

The value of an early start in moving down the pathway of localized industrial development illustrates the point well. Thus, although Santa Clara County (later to become Silicon Valley) did not offer any overwhelmingly greater locational benefits to the infant semiconductor industry than scores of other places in the United States in the mid-1950s,[19] its first-mover advantages—especially in the production of the most technologically advanced kinds of semiconductor devices —were decisive in securing its ultimate geographical domination of

---

[18] Cf. M. H. Best, *The New Competition: Institutions of Industrial Restructuring*, Cambridge: Polity Press, 1990.

[19] A. J. Scott and D. P. Angel, 'The US semiconductor industry: a locational analysis', *Environment and Planning A*, 19 (1987): 875–912.

the industry. By the mid- to late 1960s a widening stream of powerful agglomeration economies was being created in Silicon Valley, and on this basis it then moved into a position of uncontested long-run pre-eminence as a semiconductor manufacturing region. In this specific instance the early development process was for the most part a matter of chance combined perhaps with a small extra-market assist from a few active individuals associated with Stanford University. It does not seem at all probable, however, that even the most visionary of Silicon Valley's early boosters could have predicted and planned for its re-markable developmental path over the 1970s and 1980s. In other words, the unforeseeable, in both its positive and negative aspects, can be expected to be always a major element of regional development pro-cesses, and we most certainly cannot hope to construct omniscient mechanisms for steering the regional economy around every reef and shoal that may lie in its way. In spite of this proviso, we can almost always achieve better results through deliberate action than through blind faith in the infallibility of market-driven outcomes.

Consider, for instance, the household furniture industry of Los Angeles. In this particular industry, the signal absence in recent years of any apparatus for overall coordination has resulted in a situation of self-reinforcing deterioration in labor-market conditions, worker skills, and product quality.[20] A similar syndrome is represented by the once-vibrant London furniture industry which more or less collapsed during the 1960s and 1970s.[21] Yet, as I shall indicate in the next sec-tion, a number of relatively low-cost strategies of collective inter-vention can be suggested as a means of dealing with situations of this sort, and at least some amelioration might be expected to follow from their implementation. Indeed, in Los Angeles a local economic development organization, Rebuild LA, which was set up in the after-math of the 1992 riots,[22] has begun successfully to reorient selected seg-ments of the furniture industry by means of energetic network-brokering

---

[20] A. J. Scott, 'Economic decline and regeneration in a regional manufacturing com-plex: Southern California's household furniture industry', *Entrepreneurship and Regional Development*, 8 (1996): 75–98.

[21] M. H. Best, 'Sector strategies and industrial policy: the furniture industry and the Greater London Enterprise Board', in P. Hirst and J. Zeitlin (eds.), *Reversing Industrial Decline? Industrial Structure and Policy in Britain and her Competitors*, Oxford: Berg, 1989, pp. 191–222.

[22] The organization has now been absorbed into a new entity called LA Prosper Partners, a joint venture between the Community Development Technology Center, Los Angeles Community College District, and the former Rebuild LA.

activities and other collective ventures among small local manufacturers. A further example of this sort of collectively organized change process is offered by Denmark, where systematic social negotiation of general economic trends has helped to maintain high levels of prosperity over an extended time period.[23]

STRATEGIES OF REGIONAL DEVELOPMENT

Obviously, these remarks are pregnant with implications both for the analysis of spontaneous processes of social regulation in regional economic systems and for normative issues of regional development policy. They offer a very different set of tools for the pursuit of regional prosperity from those that first made their appearance as keynesian welfare-statist regional policy began to unwind in the 1970s. In the vacuum created by this collapse, a first response by local governments was a heavy reliance on entrepreneurial action in an effort above all to entice new industry to locate in their areas by means of tax holidays, fiscal incentives, attractive land deals, and so on. In some cases there were even explicit attempts to 'grow the next Silicon Valley' by these means,[24] though, from everything that has gone before, we may deduce that it will normally be inadvisable to attempt to replicate *ab initio* in one location the features of an already flourishing agglomeration in another. In any case, most of these efforts failed signally to ignite any meaningful long-run process of regional economic growth.

In the light of the present analysis, any rational approach to strategic regional economic planning should no doubt begin with an exhaustive audit of all local assets and their developmental possibilities in relation to the acquired competitive advantages of *other* regions. It should then focus intently on local institution-building, paying particular attention to the specific tasks and objectives enumerated earlier, and with a main eye always on the search for positive agglomeration economies and appropriate steering mechanisms. However, since every regional economy is in practice an idiosyncratic mix of present resources and

[23] A. Amin and D. Thomas, 'The negotiated economy: state and civic institutions in Denmark', *Economy and Society*, 25 (1996): 255–81.

[24] R-E. Miller and M. Côte, *Growing the Next Silicon Valley: A Guide for Successful Regional Planning*, Lexington, Mass.: Lexington Books, 1987.

future opportunities, there can be little in the way of routine approaches to actual implementation programs.

Successful development programs must inevitably be judicious combinations of general principle and localized compromise, reflecting the actual geography and history of each individual region. The point may be exemplified by reference, again, to the case of the Los Angeles household furniture industry. In 1993 the industry employed some 13,800 workers in close to 450 establishments (so that average establishment size was just over thirty workers); in the early 1980s the number of workers and establishments in the industry had been almost double these amounts. The main factors underlying this decline appear to be a combination of low wages, low skills, low levels of inter-firm collaboration and, as a result, low product quality. The industry cannot compete with high-quality imports; and because its wages—low as they may already be—are much higher than those of furniture workers in Latin America and Asia, it cannot compete with cheap imports either. Thus, the Los Angeles household furniture industry is facing a mounting crisis, and since it can never in the long term win the competitive battle against cheap Third World producers at the low end of the market, its best option over time would appear to be a wholesale restructuring directed toward the building of regional and firm-specific competitive advantages that might enable it to compete successfully at the top end. Unfortunately, this is a difficult objective to attain, because the quest for skill-based high-quality outputs is more risky in the immediate short term than simple wage-cutting, and it calls for more disciplined foresight on the part of individual producers. It would also presumably entail significant changes in local industrial organization and culture.

How might a negotiated transformation of the Los Angeles household furniture industry (or any other similar industry) be effected, and what specific structural/institutional features should such a transformation seek to bring into being? Figure 6.1 provides some schematized responses to this question. The figure highlights five organizational axes that together constitute the main interlocking private and public features of a prospective high-skill, high-wage, and high-quality household furniture industry in Los Angeles. Each axis may be briefly described in turn.

1. The center of Figure 6.1 designates the market, and in the present context this is taken above all to coincide with a system of

Fig. 6.1. A prospective view of a regional household furniture manufacturing system together with an associated set of institutional infrastructures

niche markets for high-quality furniture, both locally and in the rest of the world.

2. The circle drawn immediately around the market represents the main body of household furniture manufacturers in Los Angeles, but now prescriptively tied together in regional collaborative networks, which implies in turn that there is some mechanism of extra-market social organization binding participants together into cohesive units.

3. Tier 3 in the figure stands in for all the many different specialized subcontractors within the Los Angeles furniture industry. They are presumed to be fully integrated into the same collaborative networks that link manufacturers together, and, by the same token, to be working closely with manufacturers to fill orders to high standards of specification.

4. Beyond this is a fourth tier, representing the numerous design professions and complementary craft, fashion, and cultural-products industries that exist in Los Angeles, all of which offer enormous (and organizable) potential externalities on which the household furniture industry might draw, and to which in turn it might contribute.

5. The fifth and outer tier of the figure alludes to diverse agencies and institutions of collective order, some of which actually exist in Los Angeles at the present time and some of which are purely anticipatory in nature, but all of which have important roles to play in any reconstructed household furniture industry in the region, from the training of skilled labor to the provision of technology transfer services.

It need scarcely be pointed out that this outline of a possible future furniture industry in Los Angeles is signally lacking in detailed specifications; and it most certainly is not presented as a mature plan ready to be implemented. It merely begins the task of pinpointing some of the issues and questions raised by the specific problems that the industry faces at the present moment, and schematizes them in the light of the previous theoretical discussion. Even to initiate any sort of action along the lines suggested above would further presuppose a major effort of political education and mobilization among the various parties most involved in the industry today.

Notwithstanding such difficulties, this general approach is very much in practical gestation as we enter the twenty-first century, and as regions throughout the world struggle to confront the changing structures of production and competition described in these pages. No doubt, effective formulation and implementation of any meaningful action along the lines suggested would also call for the establishment of local industrial councils to work in association with local authorities, and probably even some sort of overall regional policy forum in which general problems of local strategic choice might be debated and solutions to them proposed. As such, the view of regional development advocated here has the obvious merit of seeking to marry the flexibility that resides in fragmented but multifaceted systems of production with the overall strategic competence of the large umbrella organization, thus avoiding some of the deficiencies that are associated with each of these extremes in isolation from one another.

If the analysis presented here is even partially correct, the rapidly increasing visibility of governmental and non-governmental agencies in efforts to sustain regional competitive advantage throughout the world at the present time is very much more than a passing fad. For all the reasons adduced, it appears in fact to be an early symptom of what will in all likelihood turn into a surging wave over the next decade or so.[25] This theme, and its implications for the changing political complexion of many of the world's most economically advanced regions, is taken up again in Chapter 8.

[25] Cf. P. Cooke, 'Building a twenty-first century regional economy in Emilia-Romagna', *European Planning Studies*, 4 (1996): 53–62; R. Leonardi and R. Y. Nanetti (eds.), *The Regions and European Integration: The Case of Emilia-Romagna*, London: Pinter, 1990; D. Osborne, *Laboratories of Democracy*, Boston: Harvard Business School Press, 1988.

7

Prospects for Poor Regions

THE END OF THE THIRD WORLD?

If the dynamic heartlands of global capitalism can be described in geographic terms as an interconnected mosaic of affluent regions, its extensive margins by contrast are mainly represented by a set of disjoint, impoverished spaces, many of which are increasingly falling behind in the developmental race. These extensive margins are occasionally punctuated by dense polarized centers of economic activity and population growth, some of them much overgrown in size relative to local levels of economic development. Thus, as indicated in Table 4.1, as many as ten of the fifteen largest metropolitan areas in the world (i.e. Mexico City, São Paulo, Shanghai, Bombay, Beijing, Calcutta, Buenos Aires, Seoul, Rio de Janeiro, and Tianjin) are now to be found in lesser developed countries. Nevertheless, it is precisely in such cities as these that development, when it does occur, tends to be most concentrated, and it is also through them that economic exchange between their wider national territories and the rest of the world is principally channelled.

The spatial concentration of economic development processes has in fact been a persistent feature of capitalism throughout its entire history. Pollard has shown that it was a dominant dimension of the industrial revolutions that swept over Western Europe in the eighteenth and nineteenth centuries, resulting in the massive urbanization of regions like the English Midlands, north-eastern France, Lorraine, Belgium, southern Holland, the Ruhr, Silesia, and so on.[1] Economic development in Japan at the end of the nineteenth and beginning of the twentieth centuries was similarly concentrated in geographic space, with its main axis corresponding to the belt of cities stretching from Tokyo in the north, through Nagoya, to Osaka and the Inland Sea area in the south. Even when the bases of national development

---

[1] S. Pollard, *Peaceful Conquest: The Industrialization of Europe, 1760–1970*, Oxford: Oxford University Press, 1981.

have been closely related to agriculture and resource extraction, as they were in the cases of Argentina, Australia, Brazil, Canada, New Zealand, and the Pacific North-west of the United States, large urban settlements typically emerged as the privileged centers of commercial, financial, and resource-processing activities. And, as various countries in what was then commonly referred to as the periphery began to move decisively upward in terms of per capita income levels after the mid-twentieth century, it was again largely on the basis of industrialization and urbanization in a few selected locales, such as Hong Kong, Singapore, Seoul, São Paulo, or Mexico City.

Uneven spatial development is indeed one of the great omnipresent factors that underlies economic growth as we know it. Whether we follow the neoclassical faith that simply clearing away obstacles to market penetration will secure growth, or dependency theory doctrines of import substitution, or contemporary notions about export-oriented industrialization, we are always faced with the empirical reality that growth occurs more intensely in some places than in others, and that it is primarily though not exclusively an urban phenomenon. On the few occasions when any really thoroughgoing anti-urban development strategy has been adopted, as in the Soviet Union in the 1920s or Cambodia under the Khmer Rouge, the results have usually been catastrophic, even by strictly local standards. This is not to say that agriculture or dispersed resource extraction (such as forestry) do not or cannot play positive roles in development, but it does strongly re-affirm the view that cities are a critical and indispensable part of the process. Even the relatively mild policy of polarization reversal that found favor with international development agencies in the 1980s[2] seems to have been quietly abandoned in the 1990s as newly industrializing countries have increasingly and successfully entered world export markets for manufactured goods, and as long-run growth has re-asserted itself in the primate cities of less economically developed countries.

Despite continuing stubborn cases of economic backwardness in parts of Africa, Asia, and Latin America, sustained growth has been

---

[2] H. Richardson, 'Polarization reversal in developing countries', *Papers of the Regional Science Association*, 45 (1980): 67–85; D. Rondinelli, *Secondary Cities in Developing Countries: Policies for Diffusing Urbanization*, Beverly Hills: Sage, 1983; P. M. Townroe and D. Keen, 'Polarization reversal in the state of São Paulo, Brazil', *Regional Studies*, 18 (1984): 45–54.

occurring in many areas that only a few decades ago were considered by some analysts to be irretrievably doomed to underdevelopment. Countries like Brazil, Gabon, Malaysia, Mauritius, Mexico, and South Korea are now classified in the upper tier of middle-income countries, according to World Bank definitions based on GDP per capita,[3] and Hong Kong and Singapore are now unambiguously ensconced in the high-income category, ahead of Portugal, Spain, Ireland, Australia, the United Kingdom, Italy, and even Canada.

These erstwhile Third World countries are now generally more intent on pursuing economic growth by means of export orientation (i.e. carving out viable niches for themselves in the international division of labor) than they are on achieving quasi-self-sufficiency via import substitution. But exactly because of this widespread strategic shift in development strategy, they are also faced as a policy matter with reinforcing the foundations of their local production systems and with ensuring that their competitive advantages relative to the rest of the world become ever more finely tuned. With more and more countries—and parts of countries—beginning to grow economically in this globally oriented manner, we can indeed envisage what Harris has alluded to as 'the end of the Third World',[4] signifying the cessation or at least the metamorphosis of those ideological-*cum*-political divisions that over much of the post-war decades pitted the dependent, stagnant, resource-based economies of underdeveloped areas against the prosperous manufacturing-based economies of developed areas. This older order of things is steadily giving way before a much more complex and multi-tiered system of interdependent globalization where, to be sure, vast income inequalities continue to exist, but also negotiated participation in the world economy (on certain terms, at least) can sometimes trigger significant developmental effects in economically backward areas.

One of the principal manifestations of this state of affairs today is the emergence of an expanding global mosaic of regional economies forming a new world-wide spatial division of labor. With countries like Russia, Hungary, Poland, the Ukraine, the Baltic Republics, and even China beginning to participate actively in the same system, the

---

[3] World Bank, *World Development Report*, New York: Oxford University Press (annual).
[4] N. Harris, *The End of the Third World: Newly Industrializing Countries and the Decline of an Ideology*, London: Penguin Books, 1986.

Second World too now appears more or less permanently to be passing away.

Notwithstanding the note of optimism conveyed by these remarks, it bears repeating that decent standards of living still remain a distant dream for much of the world's population. Moreover, from early nineteenth-century Manchester to contemporary Bombay, Caracas, Jakarta, or Lagos, dense spatially polarized development has always been accompanied by considerable poverty and other social costs—pollution, congestion, overcrowding, crime, stress, cultural disintegration, and so on—that typically fall disproportionately on the mass of people at the bottom of the income ladder. These problems are exacerbated by the demographic explosiveness (owing to a high ratio of births to deaths, and large-scale inmigration) and by the soaring unemployment rates that generally characterize large cities in low-income economies.[5]

INDUSTRIALIZATION, URBANIZATION, AND DEVELOPMENT

Economic development, whatever concrete form it may take in any empirical case, cannot proceed in the absence of a process of accumulation of physical and human capital. But while accumulation in this rudimentary sense may be a necessary condition of development, it is certainly not a sufficient one. At a minimum, accumulation must also be accompanied by an ancillary and evolving social scaffolding capable of sustaining effective networks of production and exchange.[6] This scaffolding includes not only operational intra-firm structures of management, labor relations, and productive activity, but also inter-firm and local labor-market institutions (rules, conventions, associations, and so on), which ensure that collective order is maintained, as well as mechanisms to provide for efficient resource allocation (which involves appropriate alignment of prices with average and marginal

---

[5] M. P. Todaro, 'Urbanization in developing nations: trends, prospects, and policies', *Journal of Geography*, 79 (1980): 164–74.

[6] D. C. North, 'The new institutional economics and Third World development', in J. Harriss, J. Hunter, and C. M. Lewis (eds.), *The New Institutional Economics and Third World Development*, London: Routledge, 1995, pp. 17–26; B. Stallings, 'The new international context of development', in B. Stallings (ed.), *Global Change, Regional Response: The New International Context of Development*, Cambridge: Cambridge University Press, 1995, pp. 349–87.

costs). Balassa has advanced a series of further factors that are critical to the rate of development in any given country, including natural resource endowments, exchange rates, preferential trade ties, foreign aid and investment, education, political conditions, and country size.[7] We may add, in view of all that has gone before, that the dense spatial concentration of production—i.e. urbanization—is also an essential moment in the entire development process under capitalism, both as an effect (because interdependent and transactions-intensive producers will tend to seek out locational proximity to one another under clearly specifiable conditions) and as a cause (because agglomeration provides performance-boosting external economies of scale and scope).

These remarks may be clarified by means of a brief examination of patterns of urbanization by country in relation to stage of economic development. In light of the previous discussion, we should expect to find that urbanization is closely and positively correlated with such indices of economic development as levels of industrialization and average income. Now refer to Table 7.1, which presents the results of a series of logistic regressions in which the dependent variable is represented by rates of urbanization across countries at all stages of development. More specifically, the rate of urbanization in any country is defined as the proportion of the total population living in all urban areas. The independent variables in this exercise, industrialization and income, are represented by (*a*) the proportion of the total national labor force occupied in industry, and (*b*) GDP per capita, respectively. Four different analyses are set forth in Table 7.1, one for all 126 countries for which data are available, and one for countries in each of three average-income categories, i.e. low-income countries (GDP per capita less than or equal to $725 per annum), middle-income countries (GDP per capita between $726 and $8,955 per annum), and high-income countries (GDP per capita greater than or equal to $8,956 per annum).

The results for the 126-country logistic regression indicate quite clearly that both the industrialization and the income variables (which are themselves statistically linked by a simple correlation coefficient of 0.39) have significantly positive impacts on urbanization, a finding that is probably fairly robust given the inconsistencies of definition that are inevitably to be found in data of the type under examination

---

[7] B. Balassa, *The Newly Industrializing Countries in the World Economy*, Oxford: Pergamon, 1981.

TABLE 7.1. Logistic regression analyses of the effects of GDP per capita and industrialization on the proportion of total population living in urban areas, 1994

Country	Constant term	Percent of labor force in industry (logarithms)		GDP per capita (logarithms)		R^2	Number of group observations
		Coefficient	*t*-value	Coefficient	*t*-value		
All	0.0133	0.3935	3.33	0.4543	7.77	0.61	126
Low-income	0.0067	0.3041	2.77	0.6136	3.77	0.51	48
Middle-income	0.0061	0.8401	3.23	0.3596	2.17	0.27	55
High-income	0.3305	1.2227	0.65	0.6900	0.83	0.05	23

Note: The form of the regressions is representable as $p = a(\exp\Sigma b_i X_i)/(1 + a\exp\Sigma b_i X_i)$, where p is the proportion of population living in urban areas for any given country, X_i is the ith independent variable, and a and b_i are computed parameters.

Source: The analysis is based on data taken from: World Bank, *World Development Report*, New York: Oxford University Press, 1996.

here. However, the force of these correlations tends to decline as the level of development rises. As the table indicates, they are strong for low-income countries taken as a separate group, modestly strong for middle-income countries, and weak among high-income countries. Modulations of this sort are actually to be expected, given that the urbanization process as defined is eventually subject to saturation at the upper level, and that urban production systems in high-income countries tend in any case to be marked by conspicuous absolute and relative shifts away from industry and into services. The form of the regressions employed here casts urbanization as the dependent variable, though the causalities at play probably run in both directions between the dependent and independent variables. What we can say with assurance at this stage is that there are forceful (but not yet fully identified) interdependencies between urbanization, industrial development, and average income levels in less developed countries.[8]

This affirmation, of course, is entirely in line with the overall tenor of earlier arguments—even though these are for the most part addressed to issues of regional development in the more developed parts of the world. There is in principle, however, no reason why the spatial development dynamics based on agglomeration and increasing returns effects which I have claimed operate in high-income countries should not also be found in low-income and middle-income countries. Indeed, if economic activity in the latter countries is organized in interdependent transactions-intensive networks (whether in the modern sector or in more traditional, artisanal sectors) together with dense local labor-market activity, then we would anticipate spatial clustering to be strongly in evidence at selected locations. This anticipation is actually made more forceful in view of the relative scarcity of investment funds for capital-intensive urban infrastructure in less developed countries, so that suitable sites for dense industrial activity are usually fairly limited in number. Agglomeration will be accentuated yet again where local products are also successfully contesting wider national and international markets, thus increasing opportunities for expansion of the social division of labor in the home region.

To be sure, there are many possible variations on this theme, in the developing as in the developed parts of the world, as local,

---

[8] This point is stressed by N. Harris, *City, Class, and Trade: Social and Economic Change in the Third World*, London: I. B. Tauris, 1991, as well as by N. Kaldor, 'The case for regional policies', *Scottish Journal of Political Economy*, 17 (1970): 337–48.

national, and global economic forces come into conjunction with one another in given places. In Brazil, the economic miracle of the 1970s was largely accomplished by means of a national policy of import substitution, with industrial growth being concentrated above all in the greater São Paulo region.[9] In South Korea, growth was driven forward by large-scale *chaebol* enterprises operating under the umbrella of a highly interventionist and authoritarian central government,[10] and here too, the result has been an extremely uneven pattern of spatial development, with almost 50% of all manufacturing employment in the country occurring in the Seoul–Inchon region. In the new generation of electronics assembly complexes in South-east Asia (in Penang, Kuala Lumpur, Bangkok, Manila, and elsewhere) an explosion of productive activity has occurred based on the availability of cheap labor, indigenous entrepreneurial effort, and the branch plants of multinational corporations which have increasingly tended to put out specialized work to nearby subcontractors, thus helping to stimulate rounds of local growth.[11] Similarly, the burgeoning software industry in Bangalore, India, owes much of its recent dynamism to the ready availability of cheap labor, both skilled and unskilled, as well as to the subcontract orders now pouring into the region from the United States and elsewhere.

One of the most remarkable trends in many low- and middle-income countries in recent years has been the spontaneous rise of successful industrialization programs based on artisanal labor, low barriers to entry, small firms, and local know-how and culture.[12] In much of the post-war literature on development, this type of industrial activity was more or less seen as being antithetical to economic progress. It was for the most part consigned to the realm of the backward and archaic as something that impeded the forward march of modernization and

[9] M. Storper, *Industrialization, Economic Development and the Regional Question in the Third World*, London: Pion, 1991.

[10] A. H. Amsden, *Asia's Next Giant: South Korea and Late Industrialization*, New York: Oxford University Press, 1992.

[11] J. Henderson, *The Globalisation of High-Technology Production: Society, Space and Semiconductors in the Restructuring of the Modern World*, London: Routledge, 1989; A. J. Scott, 'The semiconductor industry in South East Asia: organization, location, and the international division of labor', *Regional Studies*, 21 (1987): 143–59.

[12] B. Späth, 'Small firms in Latin America: prospects for economic and socially viable development?' in B. Späth (ed.), *Small Firms and Development in Latin America*, Geneva: International Institute for Labour Studies, 1993, pp. 1–37; M. Storper, 'Territorial development in the global learning economy: the challenge to developing economies', *Review of International Political Economy*, 2 (1995): 394–424.

would no doubt be swept away as some purely mythical rationalist–universalist state of social being ushered in *real* development.[13] The frame of mind from which such notions sprang is doubtless understandable, given their historical context. Over much of the present century, production based on large-scale, capital-intensive, electromechanical technologies has been widely taken to be one of the teleological end-points of the process of economic evolution, with fordist mass production representing the most advanced concrete realization of this vision. One of the great merits of the flexible specialization thesis as set forth by Piore and Sabel in 1984[14] was that, flawed as it was in certain of its details, it opened up alternative conceptual and practical prospects that had been largely closed off by earlier theoretical commitments. The Piore–Sabel thesis stimulated a major re-evaluation of the development process by making it now reasonable to envisage the possibility of economic take-off on the basis of small-scale, labor-intensive, and even traditional forms of industry such as clothing, furniture, ceramics, jewelry, toys, kitchen utensils, and so on. In fact, in the 1950s and 1960s the early flowering of industry in Hong Kong and Singapore (two places that have unmistakably escaped from their earlier status as peripheral Third World entrepôts) had in large degree been based on just such sectors as these, though the relevant lessons were evidently not widely understood by development theorists at the time.

In recent years, these types of flexibly specialized industries have proliferated greatly in both the developed and less developed parts of the world, and a spate of case studies focusing on their regional dimensions has appeared in the scholarly literature. In the developed world (as exemplified most dramatically by the classic case of the Third Italy, which was the source of much of Piore and Sabel's inspiration) regional clusters of flexibly specialized industries have multiplied rapidly since the early 1970s. Often, though assuredly not always (as the previously discussed case of the Los Angeles furniture industry demonstrates), they are devoted to the production of high-quality outputs that compete successfully in global niche markets. In the less developed parts of the world, such clusters are more commonly spe-

---

[13] Cf. R. Redfield and M. B. Singer, 'The cultural role of cities', *Economic Development and Cultural Change*, 3 (1954): 53–73.

[14] M. J. Piore and C. F. Sabel, *The Second Industrial Divide: Possibilities for Prosperity*, New York: Basic Books, 1984.

cialized in products that compete at the lower end of the quality scale and make use to an overwhelming degree of abundant local supplies of cheap labor.

Published case studies of this phenomenon in low-income and middle-income countries now abound. Not all of these cases are likely to be viable over the long run, but all of them display at least in incipient form the multifaceted organizational patterns and associated social infrastructures that are the essential foundation of regional competitive advantage. Aero has written about traditional woodworking and furniture-making in Makambako in Tanzania, where the industry appears to be poised at the early stages of growth based on an emerging social division of labor.[15] Amorim has shown how a thriving small-scale furniture industry has developed in São João do Aruaru in north-east Brazil, partly with aid provided by the local state government.[16] Cawthorne has described the cotton knitwear industry of Tiruppur, south India, now a major manufacturing center exhibiting a mix of large and small firms combined together in tightly organized transactional networks, and complemented by large numbers of home-workers (most of them women); the entire knitwear complex provides employment for almost 30,000 workers.[17] In the northern suburbs of Kumasi, Ghana, as Dawson has indicated, a flourishing collection of industrial districts focused on carpentry, metal working, and vehicle repair has come into existence.[18] The artisanal garment industry of Quito, Ecuador, is now one of the largest manufacturing sectors in the country according to Lawson; over the 1980s the industry experienced a major crisis, the response to which has been greatly increased subcontracting out to female homeworkers.[19] In Peru, Villarán has proposed a new kind of development strategy based on localized clusters of small businesses, and he has illustrated his argument by

[15] A. Aero, 'New pathways to industrialization in Tanzania: theoretical and strategic considerations', *IDS Bulletin*, 23/3 (1992): 15–20.

[16] M. A. Amorim, 'Lessons on demand', *Technology Review*, January (1994): 30–6.

[17] P. Cawthorne, 'The labour process under amoebic capitalism: a case study of the garment industry in a south Indian town', in I. S. A. Baud and G. A. De Bruijne (eds.), *Gender, Small-Scale Industry, and Development Policy*, London: IT Publications, 1993, pp. 47–75.

[18] J. Dawson, 'The relevance of the flexible specialization paradigm for small-scale industrial restructuring in Ghana', *IDS Bulletin*, 23/3 (1992): 34–44.

[19] V. Lawson, 'Beyond the firm: restructuring gender divisions of labor in Quito's garment industry under austerity', *Environment and Planning D: Society and Space*, 13 (1995): 415–44.

reference to the clothing and metallurgical industries of Lima and the footwear industry of Trujillo.[20]

More generally, Nadvi and Schmitz have recently put together a widely ranging review of the experiences of industrial clusters in Africa, Asia, and Latin America; they indicate that the more success-ful of these clusters—much as in the case of the celebrated industrial districts of the Third Italy—tend to be characterized by a fourfold pat-tern of (*a*) specialization and complementarity (i.e. vertical disintegra-tion), (*b*) horizontal cooperation among firms, (*c*) a sustaining fabric of local social and cultural relations, and (*d*) appropriate governmental programs.[21]

Schmitz's study of the shoe industry in and around Novo Hamburgo in the state of Rio Grande do Sul, Brazil, adds further detail to these observations.[22] Schmitz describes how the industry grew out of a tra-ditional craft manufacturing cluster based on the availability of leather hides from surrounding rural areas. The Novo Hamburgo complex today contains a number of large producers employing 2,000–3,000 workers, but the majority of producers are small and are tied together in extensive social divisions of labor (see Table 7.2). The footwear industry proper in the region employs some 70,000 workers in 480 firms, mainly specializing in women's shoes. However, the footwear production chain as a whole, including upstream and auxiliary activ-ities, employs a total of 153,400 workers in 1,821 firms. Largely on the basis of the Novo Hamburgo industrial cluster, Brazil's share of world trade in leather shoes has increased from 0.5% in 1970 to 12.3% in 1990, and it now ranks third in importance after Italy and South Korea. Schmitz also documents the formation of an infrastructure of supporting institutions in Novo Hamburgo, including local training cen-ters, technical schools, industry associations, and the periodic National Shoe Fair.

In these and scores of other instances, alternative pathways to industrialization and regional growth are being opened up in many

---

[20] F. Villarán, 'Small-scale industry efficiency groups in Peru', in B. Späth (ed.), *Small Firms and Development in Latin America*, Geneva: International Institute for Labour Studies, 1993, pp. 158–95.

[21] K. Nadvi and H. Schmitz, 'Industrial clusters in less developed countries: review of experiences and research agenda', Discussion Paper no. 339, Institute of Development Studies, University of Sussex, Brighton, 1994.

[22] H. Schmitz, 'Small shoemakers and fordist giants: tale of a supercluster', *World Development*, 23 (1995): 9–28.

TABLE 7.2. The footwear industry cluster in and around Novo Hamburgo, Rio Grande do Sul, Brazil, 1991

Sector	Employment	Firms
Footwear	70,000	480
Service-rendering industries—workshops	18,000	710
Tanning	22,000	135
Leather and footwear machines	3,600	45
Components	28,000	223
Rubber	1,900	26
Leather articles	4,900	52
Export and forwarding agents	2,000	70
Others	3,000	80
Total	153,400	1,821

Source: H. Schmitz, 'Small shoemakers and fordist giants: tale of a supercluster', *World Development*, 23 (1995): 11.

less-developed countries, and in important ways, as we shall now see, these pathways provide major opportunities for policy-makers to help accelerate the process of development. Much, of course, also depends on the overarching context of national economic and political affairs, and on the long-term prospects for social order.

REGION-BASED APPROACHES TO ECONOMIC DEVELOPMENT

The previous discussion represents something of an antidote to those grim radical views, prevalent in the 1960s and 1970s, that took under-development to be a condition that is inscribed durably onto the geo-graphy of the capitalist world system, and concomitantly, as something that can be dealt with only by heroic efforts of political opposition to the North.[23] It also goes against the grain of the vacuous neo-classical faith that markets will equalize all inequalities if simply left to themselves. I most certainly do not want to minimize the difficul-ties that low- and middle-income countries face in their continuing efforts to improve living standards for all, or to suggest that the de-veloped economies represent an unequivocally benign force in the background to these efforts. Nor do I wish to claim that markets offer no useful instruments of economic organization in the quest for devel-opment. At the same time, I have no intention of suggesting that broad issues of economic development can be unproblematically assimilated into the question of regional development *tout court*. On the contrary, detailed examination of macroeconomics and the structure of social relations must remain a key element of any attempt to understand development.

Yet economic development is never geographically uniform; it tends to be concentrated in and to diffuse outward from distinctive points on the landscape, and whatever the social costs of polarized develop-ment in poor countries may be, it is almost always generative rather than parasitic on balance, to use the terminology of Hoselitz.[24] More-over, if low wages is one of the major problems of less-developed countries, the irony is that the same problem offers certain strategic

[23] For a critical summary of these views see S. Corbridge, *Capitalist World Development: A Critique of Radical Development Geography*, London: Macmillan, 1986.
[24] B. Hoselitz, 'Generative and parasitic cities', *Economic Development and Cultural Change*, 3 (1954): 278–94.

possibilities to policy-makers (and in some cases virtually the only strategic possibility) for its own resolution. That is to say, cheap labor offers these countries a definite competitive advantage which, in combination with determined efforts to build strong institutional frameworks of collective economic order at certain privileged locations, can sometimes help to launch development. In a word, the complex composite attributes and agglomeration economies of polarized regional production systems provide a number of significant policy levers that can be manipulated in the search for developmental effects, in addition to the usual approaches based on macroeconomic prescriptions.

The main sense of what is at stake here has already been conveyed in Chapter 5. The goal is to forge production complexes in specific regional contexts that have the ability to develop and grow incrementally over time *as systemic entities with endogenous increasing returns effects*. Once again, there can be no a priori recipe that will automatically deliver the desired results, though the analytical lenses constructed at an earlier stage immediately suggest some important policy tools. Thus, close attention needs to be paid to forms of intervention that seem likely to enhance local technological capacities, agglomeration-specific skills and worker aptitudes, collaborative networks enabling producers to attain to improved levels of competitive performance by means of continual combination and re-combination of their individually held assets, marketing and export promotion of regional products, the provision of modest capital loan programs for entrepreneurs, and so on. We must also add to this list of possible forms of policy intervention the critical need for institution-building in the interests of overall strategic steering of the regional economy, and for the elaboration of communal forums to deal with issues of general concern to all participants in the local economy.

In contrast to the strategy of import substitution, this kind of approach to development is presumably a relatively low-cost one since it diverts the focus of action away from massive investments in large-capital projects and toward political mobilization around the social infrastructures of production and the regional learning economy. One of its guiding principles is to build primarily on local assets (even where these consist of no more than cheap labor or primitive networks of artisanal firms) in an effort to ignite a process of cumulative causation.

It goes without saying that a major obstacle to any such effort, and one that is largely outside the sphere of social control for regions seeking to gear up their economies from a low basis of development, is that the increasing-returns effects already securely captured by more developed regions make it hard for late starters to compete. In this sense, the infant industry problem in low-income countries is doubly problematical. Not only are these countries faced with a situation where first-mover advantages are likely to be consistently pre-empted by more developed regions, but it is also difficult for them to overcome the disadvantage of their relatively low thresholds of scale and scope. Less-developed countries and regions, as already intimated, typically try to compensate for these drawbacks by specializing in forms of production that are able to benefit from large local surpluses of labor. The difficult maneuver, then—and notwithstanding the pessimism of Lewis, who believed that no increase in the income of laborers could be achieved until the surplus is absorbed[25]—is, as Hong Kong, Singapore, Brazil, Mexico, Malaysia, or Thailand have done at various points over the last few decades, to use this point of departure as a means of beginning to move up the labor-skill and product-quality gradients. This can be accomplished only if producers also have the capacity, among other things, to exploit subtle shifts in worldwide demand structures by continually differentiating their products and readjusting their positions in global commodity chains. This is precisely what some of the more successful of the newly industrializing countries have been able to achieve in a wide variety of producer- and consumer-goods industries, ranging from printed circuit boards to artificial flowers.

The current structure of the international footwear industry further exemplifies the point. With Italy having shifted largely into high-price, high-fashion shoe production, Spain is now specializing in medium-price shoes, Taiwan in plastic footwear, South Korea in athletic shoes, and Brazil in low-price women's leather shoes.[26] Presumably, many more market niches in footwear, and in a multiplicity of other products, will make their appearance as globalization continues its onward course, thus offering a yet wider range of economic opportunities for firms and regions in less developed parts of the world.

In recent years, international agencies like the World Bank and the

---

[25] A. Lewis, 'Economic development with unlimited supplies of labour', *Manchester School of Economic and Social Studies*, 22 (1954): 139–91.

[26] G. Gereffi, 'Global production systems and third world development', in B. Stallings (ed.), *Global Change, Regional Response: The New International Context of Development*, Cambridge: Cambridge University Press, 1995, pp. 100–42.

International Monetary Fund have largely abandoned their former support for import substitution as the preferred pathway to economic development.[27] They have turned instead to neo-liberal approaches posited on reductions in levels of public ownership, the encouragement of more intense forms of economic competition and market discipline, and assertive export promotion. These approaches seem to have been attended with some technical success in a number of cases, although like the shock therapy that was prescribed for the former Soviet Union and its satellites, they also bring in their train many social hardships and dysfunctionalities. The argument that I am proposing in these pages shares with the World Bank–IMF perspective a due respect for the efficiency-seeking properties of markets, but it also recognizes the need to pay close attention to the social bases of production in all their complexity. As such, the argument points toward forms of economic development that are not only potentially less damaging from a social perspective, but also more effective economically, and in which cooperation, collaboration, and regard for the well-being of the labor force are just as important as—if not more important than—simply getting prices right. The equivalent idea was admirably expressed by Hirschman some four decades ago when he wrote:

Development depends not so much on finding optimal combinations for given resources and factors of production as on calling forth and enlisting for development purposes resources and abilities that are hidden, scattered, or badly utilized.[28]

The ultimate objective is to establish thriving regional economies whose products can compete convincingly in world markets, and then to use this acquired capability as the basis for programmed expansion of their stocks of agglomeration economies. As suggested by the information presented earlier in Figures 4.1 and 4.2, there are numerous regions in the less developed parts of the world—most especially in middle-income countries—that are already some part of the the way to becoming fully fledged motors of the new global economy. Unfortunately, there are also many perplexing cases of left-behinds and castaways in the world's poorest areas that seem likely, at least for the foreseeable future, to remain stubbornly resistant to economic development efforts of any sort.

---

[27] See, e.g. H. Stein, 'Deindustrialization, adjustment, the World Bank, and the IMF in Africa', *World Development*, 20 (1992): 83–95.

[28] A. Hirschman, *The Strategy of Economic Development*, New Haven: Yale University Press, p. 5.

8

A World of Regions

NEW POLITICAL SPACES

The forces now reshaping the economic geography of the world are bound up with many concurrent trends of political reorganization reflecting deficits of governance at virtually every major point of articulation in the world economy. These political trends, however, often lag behind the economic changes to which they are in part a response. One consequence of this lag—and especially in view of the virtual demise of national keynesian–welfare-statist policy-making—is that the resulting vacuum is often by default taken over by a market-driven logic, even though this logic sometimes undermines the possibility of attaining alternative social goals. For example, and especially in regional contexts, it can lead to competitive contests and rivalries that when left unchecked may corrode those subtle processes of association, co-operation, and communal solidarity that are critical to much economic success and social welfare in the contemporary world.[1] There are therefore urgent political tasks that need to be attended to as the present economic conjuncture evolves, and as the need for robust social regulation at all levels of economic interaction becomes more pressing. This need is not just a technocratic policy imperative, but also a call to political mobilization, for some of the most basic human rights and liberties are also at stake in the economic and political changes that are now in course on all sides.

The political reorganization of the world that is coming into clearer outline as we enter the twenty-first century can be understood schematically in terms of a fourfold hierarchy of governance relations as indicated in Figure 8.1. Every tier in this hierarchy represents an important nexus of socio-spatial relationships posing complex policy problems. The main features of each tier may be concisely summarized as follows.

---

[1] Cf. M. Albert, *Capitalisme Contre Capitalisme*, Paris: Editions du Seuil, 1991.

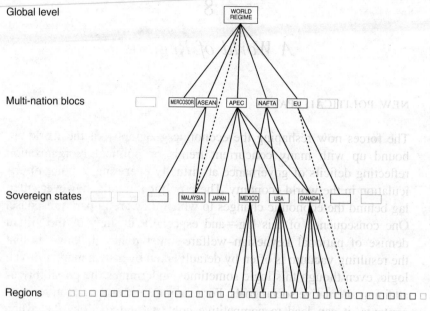

FIG. 8.1. Fragment of an emerging global hierarchy of economic and political relations

1. The top of the hierarchy consists of an emerging global regime made up by supra-national organizations, international agreements, diplomatic conventions, and so on. As politically flimsy and disjointed as this regime may be at the present time, it has come into existence in response to a critical set of regulatory stresses in the global arena. It is here that efforts to construct forums for the coordination of exchange rates, the supervision of multinational corporations, the management of intellectual property rights, the surveillance of international environmental and health conditions, and so on are gradually being focused. As things now stand, the ability of the global regime to carry out these functions is strictly limited, but in view of the arguments deployed earlier in Chapter 3, it seems reasonable to suppose that it may become more politically effective in the future. However, the precise institutional format that it will ultimately assume (e.g. a floating system of international contracts; a new concert of nations; world government) remains entirely a matter of speculation at this stage.

2. Below this top tier is ranged a layer of economico-political units consisting of multi-nation blocs such as the European Union (EU), the North American Free Trade Association (NAFTA), and the Organization for Asia-Pacific Economic Cooperation (APEC). The number of these organizations has grown rapidly since the 1950s when the first steps toward Western European integration were taken.[2] If few of them have much real economic and political weight at the present time, they can be seen as a response to the ever-increasing demand for orderly governance at the supra-national level, and a response to the call for accelerated growth by means of intra-bloc free exchange and more finely grained divisions of labor (whence, also, augmented economies of scale in production). In addition, the limited number of participant countries in any one instance ensures some modicum of overall manageability. Again, it seems reasonable to assume that the individual units at this level in the global hierarchy will in the normal course of events continue to consolidate their role as centers of authority and influence.

3. The third level in the hierarchy is made up of sovereign states, which are still by far the most potent distillations of economic and political power in the modern world. Even so, and to repeat a familiar

---

[2] J. H. Mittelman, 'Rethinking the new regionalism in the context of globalization', *Global Governance*, 2 (1996): 189–213.

refrain, there is an increasing spatial mismatch between the sovereign state as such and the organizational features of modern capitalism. As a result, many of the regulatory economic functions of the sovereign state are now passing upward in the hierarchy to the multinational and global levels as capitalism itself becomes similarly reconstituted in various ways. Equally, many functions are passing downward, for the resurgence of the region in modern capitalism opens up numerous new demands and opportunities for regulatory and political action at sub-national tiers of governance.

4. Hence, the fourth and final level of the hierarchy is constituted by a large group of individual regions forming a complex global mosaic. Each of these regions represents a more or less advanced assemblage of economic and social activities formed in response to the centripetal dynamic of agglomeration. In the traditional sovereign territorial state, regions necessarily function as subordinate administrative units whose range of activities is a reflection of the balance between centralization and devolution that is struck in any given national context. With the erosion that now appears to be going on in the regulatory capacities of the sovereign state, however—so that the state in its classical form looks more and more not like an absolute but a transitory historical phenomenon[3]—a space is clearly opening up in which regions are becoming the sites of important, if not radical, local administrative initiatives and political activities independently of the level above.

Three further general points need to be stressed in regard to the schema laid out in Figure 8.1.

First, and to a steadily increasing extent, the individual units comprising any level in the hierarchy are subject to multiple and overlapping allegiances in their relations to units at the next higher level. This means, for example, that any region (such as one of the newly materializing trans-border regions of Western Europe, North America, or East and South-east Asia) may lie within the jurisdiction of more than one sovereign state.

Second, there are numerous short-circuits between non-adjacent tiers. Accordingly, regions can and often do have direct unmediated relations with the representatives of multi-nation blocs, thus bypassing the level of the sovereign state; and sovereign states can and systematically do

---

[3] J-M. Guéhenno, *La Fin de la Démocratie*, Paris: Flammarion, 1993.

make interventions at the global level without invoking the collaboration of the multi-nation blocs to which they belong. Nowhere has the process of the direct interpellation of the representatives of the multi-nation bloc by individual regions gone further than in the European Union. Here, a Committee of the Regions, comprising a total of 222 members, has been established under the terms of the Maastricht Treaty, with the objective of giving local authorities a clear voice in the formulation of EU policies and in the administration of its affairs; if the powers of the Committee are still somewhat provisional, they will undoubtedly expand with the passage of time.

Third, while the individual units composing the different tiers of the hierarchy sketched out in Figure 8.1 are all identified in terms of specifically *spatial* aggregates, there are numerous instances where the relevant communities of interest, together with their formal and informal institutional representations, are in fact arranged along more functional lines (for example the multinational corporation, industrial sectors and their representative associations, trade and worker alliances, scientific bodies, many different kinds of social organizations). Thus, Figure 8.1 maps out only a partial though a significant set of the total range of social and regulatory possibilities in the modern world.

Each level in this hierarchy is marked by numerous problematical issues that are unique to it. Each level, accordingly, offers a special assortment of opportunities for political organization and the concretization of democratic principles,[4] though the sovereign state continues to function as the privileged hub of all such opportunities at the present time. More generally, the units in any tier in the hierarchy are never just simple microcosms of units at higher tiers. Yet at all levels in the hierarchy there are also many common and recurrent political questions (e.g. about trade, workers' rights, gender issues, the environment, political representation). In view of this, and especially given the continuing extension and integration of capitalism throughout the horizontal and vertical dimensions of the hierarchy—often in ways that evade any sort of democratic scrutiny—there is perhaps now more than ever a pressing need for revivified mass political movements with coordinated forms of expression at all levels. One of the urgent tasks of any such movement as we enter

---

[4] D. Held, *Democracy and the Global Order: From the Modern State to Cosmopolitan Governance*, Stanford, Calif.: Stanford University Press, 1996.

the twenty-first century is to harness economic progress to social and cultural needs, in opposition to the frequent subordination of those same needs to the logic of the market as the pace of globalization picks up.

REGIONAL DIRECTORATES OF THE TWENTY-FIRST CENTURY?

The intra-regional dimension

Local government in one form or another is a universal feature of political apparatuses in the modern world. It exists both as an instrument for filtering central government mandates down to the local level (e.g. in such matters as education, justice, or public health) and as a locus of authority for dealing with administrative issues whose territorial expression is typically confined to a relatively narrow area (e.g. the provision of urban services, or the treatment of localized market failures such as traffic congestion, land-development bottlenecks, and urban blight).[5] In some countries, especially those with a unitary political tradition, like Britain or Japan, local government is in practice relatively weak; in others, especially those with federal constitutions, such as Canada, Germany, or the United States, it is relatively strong, and some genuine degree of local sovereignty can usually be said to exist. Within the framework of the classical sovereign state, however, local government is always contained by and subordinate to the political authority of the center, which is also the fountainhead of citizenship and national identity as well as the source of macro-economic order. In the advanced capitalist societies, local government as we have known it is the offspring of the sovereign state and of national economic imperatives.

The concomitant problem is that most existing forms of local government are not particularly well equipped to deal with the complexities of regional economic governance in post-fordist, post-keynesian, globalizing capitalism. To be sure, the traditional tasks of local government (including urban and regional planning) remain as pressing as ever. But clearly, new and urgent demands for civic action are erupting on all sides, and the decision-making mandates and administrative arrangements that are typically to be found at the local level

---

[5] A. J. Scott, *The Urban Land Nexus and the State*, London: Pion, 1980.

are simply not designed to respond effectively to these demands. Above and beyond local government as usual, what appears most to be required at the present time is the construction of supplementary forums and mechanisms of collective action capable of dealing with the subtle tasks of local regulation in a world where economic affairs are to such a large extent constituted as place-bound networks of production and labor-market activity intimately caught up within wider economic networks, often cutting indiscriminately across the boundaries of the traditional sovereign state. In many respects, this requirement is in fact now beginning to call into being an enormously varied range of responses throughout the world, so that, even though politically conservative currents continue to remain dominant in the sphere of economic policy-making, the lineaments of a new approach now seem to be surfacing, and nowhere is this more the case than at the local level.

These responses revolve generally around initiatives to deal with the complex collective order that is an intrinsic quality of all regional economic systems. This order consists of localized social and economic interactions that when appropriately coordinated engender streams of positive externalities, thus providing competitive advantages for all. Since this domain of externalities lies by definition beyond the discretionary control of any private agent, relevant forms of social—though not necessarily governmental—coordination are essential if the best possible performance of the regional economy is to be secured. As indicated earlier, these externalities crop up in a bewildering variety of practical contexts ranging from inter-firm subcontracting relations to collective learning processes, and from local labor markets to customary forms of economic competition and collaboration. Because every regional production system together with its mantle of externalities is locked into a path-dependent process of evolution, and since markets alone cannot guarantee automatic selection of socially optimal long-term trajectories of development, some sort of strategic guidance of the local economy is also to be commended despite the evident difficulties of constructing a set of administrative tools that have the right kinds of sensitivity and flexibility. These *desiderata* are doubly compelling in a world where rapidly augmenting cross-border flows of goods and services put regions throughout the global mosaic in a situation of head-to-head competition with one another, and where national governments can no longer be relied upon unfailingly to provide protection or aid to those regions that begin to falter. Once more it should be stressed that, even though the broad specifications of the regional question in an expanding global economy can be described with some generality, each particular region is always a unique combination of empirical circumstances, so that meaningful political responses to the predicaments described above will invariably require detailed tailoring to match local conditions.

In spite of the uniqueness of every individual region, certain generic features of the new political arrangements that are taking shape at least in embryonic form in many regions today can be fairly easily deciphered; and these arrangements are predictably on the agenda everywhere as regional economic dilemmas intensify. I use the term *regional directorate* to refer to the prospective political apparatuses that are being ushered in by these changes. It is tempting to appropriate the more dramatic expression *city-state* or even Ohmae's neologism *region-state*[6] to designate what I have in mind here, but the temptation is in the end to be resisted in view of the resonances of the term 'state' with all of its accumulated meanings focused on a self-contained and sovereign structure of governance representing the condensation of society as a whole. More specifically, I mean by a regional directorate a system of local control and coordination made up of any combination of formal governmental agencies, civil associations and organizations, and private–public partnerships that, in addition to carrying out the usual tasks of territorial administration, has at least some of the following features:

1. a modicum of organizational coherence, internal coordination, and independence;
2. sufficient legitimacy and authority to negotiate and monitor collectively beneficial agreements about forms of local social regulation of the production system and labor markets as a whole;
3. the political ability and financial resources to build institutions cutting across the grain of the local economy so as to ensure that increasing-returns effects that would otherwise be dissipated are potentiated and captured for the benefit of all;
4. the organizational and analytical capacity to establish policy frameworks and guidelines providing strategic temporal guidance for the entire regional economy;

---

[6] K. Ohmae, *The End of the Nation State*, New York: Free Press, 1995.

5. the warrant to engage in meaningful encounters with other regional directorates in other parts of the world in pursuit of mutual economic and social harmonization.

These propositions are purely suggestive, and I consciously make no attempt to elaborate on the details about how they might be operationalized in practice, or about the substantive consequences (social as well as economic) that might ensue from any attempt to put them into concrete execution; and I defer until later any commentary on the critical question of whose interests may or may not be served as a result. The propositions are presented as an amalgam of theoretical inference and futurological conjecture, and like all such propositions they are perhaps best left in a rough-hewn state as long as a high proportion of their meaning is purely speculative. This is the same as saying that, while something generally of the order described in points 1–5 above may be decipherable in the tea-leaves of the present, the actual historical unfolding of events on the ground is apt to be infinitely more complex, problematical, and indeterminate.

In particular, I avoid any effort to predict or prescribe the precise territorial configuration of individual regional directorates, should they ever materialize in practice. What can be said with confidence is that, if something approximating them does indeed come empirically into existence, they are most likely to be physically anchored in dense polarized clusters of economic activity coinciding with one or more metropolitan areas and a variable stretch of hinterland, akin to the regional motors mapped out in Figure 4.2. However, like social classes in Thompson's view of history, we may expect their actual shape (both functionally and spatially) to be forged in the cut and thrust of political practice.[7] As such, their specifically territorial outlines are liable to reflect intricate processes of spatial competition and alliance-making between adjacent areas.

A striking instance of a local authority that has successfully engaged in the active extension and consolidation of its political domain is the city of Lille in France. Under the visionary leadership of its mayor, Pierre Mauroy, Lille went through a major economic restructuring over the 1970s and 1980s, becoming a major node on

---

[7] E. P. Thompson, *The Making of the English Working Class*, London: Victor Gollancz, 1963.

the northern European *train à grande vitesse* network, and then using this decisive advantage to exert growing influence within a tri-national region spreading over much of Nord-Pas-de-Calais, Flanders, and (via the Channel Tunnel) Kent.

However, we are obviously very far indeed at the present time from the achievement of full-blown regional directorates of the sort alluded to above. Hong Kong (before 1 July 1997?), Singapore, and Taiwan might be taken as flourishing advance cases of what is possible, though it seems improbable that sovereign states would ever voluntarily relinquish control over their component regions to the point where entire countries in effect break up into a series of smaller independent units. Still, over the last few decades local governmental apparatuses have tended not only to become more highly developed and more aggressively effective, but also to probe more and more widely into new domains of activity, many of them involving forms of economic policy-making hitherto largely beyond the competence of local authorities. In a number of instances, something even approaching regional strategic trade policies seems to be in the offing as regions seek to build the foundations of vibrant local economies focused on export production, and then to engage actively in the commercialization and marketing of these exports in foreign countries.

Examples of these tendencies abound in the new 'Europe of the regions', where official EU policy is much focused not only on top-down measures to reduce geographical disparities, but also on facilitating bottom-up deployment of local economic and political resources, and where regions are becoming major arenas of political dialogue and action.[8] Specific cases can be found in the German *länder*, with their elaborate private–public consultative and decision-making machinery and their ambitious industrial development programs;[9] in Italy, where the strong local governments created by the reforms of the

---

[8] M. Keating, 'Europeanism and regionalism', in B. Jones and M. Keating (eds.), *The European Union and the Regions*, Oxford: Clarendon Press, 1995, pp. 1–22; R. J. Bennett and G. Krebs, 'Local economic development partnerships: an analysis of policy networks in EC–LEDA local employment development strategies', *Regional Studies*, 28 (1994): 119–40.

[9] P. Cooke and K. Morgan, *Industry, Training and Technology Transfer: The Baden–Württemberg System in Perspective*, Cardiff: Regional Industrial Research, 1990; G. Herrigel, 'Large firms, small firms, and the governance of flexible specialization: the case of Baden–Württemberg and socialized risk', in B. Kogut (ed.), *Country Competitiveness: Technology and the Organization of Work*, New York: Oxford University Press, 1993, pp. 15–35.

1970s promote technological innovation, labor training, market research, export activity, information sharing, and so on, and where indeed a breakaway regional movement in the form of the Lega Nord even threatens the geographical integrity of the country as a whole;[10] in the Belgian confederate system, where the three regions of Flanders, Wallonia, and the Brussels Metropolitan Region are to all intents and purposes autonomous in all domains of social and industrial policy; and more embryonically in the seventeen autonomous communities of Spain, or the twenty-two elected regional councils of France.[11]

In the United States, too, the existing framework of local government has grown strongly relative to the federal government over the last couple of decades. Some of this growth can be seen as a means of executing (and depoliticizing) the retreat on the part of federal government from its former predilection for keynesian welfare-statist policy. Some of it is also an authentic response to the economic tensions and predicaments that are now so strongly evident at the local level, and that have been in part unleashed by the self-same retreat of the federal government from its earlier commitments. Most especially, numerous social experiments are currently in progress in almost all of the states and large metropolitan areas in the United States (notably in California, Massachusetts, Michigan, New York, and Pennsylvania), involving the formulation and implementation of far-reaching economic development programs. These have been established with various goals in mind: to encourage the formation of local business networks, to set up new technology alliances, to train workers, to promote regional products, to secure first-mover advantages in certain strategic industries, and in general to stimulate the formation of virtuous circles of cumulative causation.

At the same time, throughout the world, and perhaps most of all in the United States, there has been an efflorescence of para-governmental and civil organizations of many different varieties seeking to provide governance services for the local economy.[12] One such organization

[10] P. Bianchi, 'Levels of policy and the nature of post-fordist competition', in M. Storper and A. J. Scott (eds.), *Pathways to Industrialization and Regional Development*, London: Routledge, 1993, pp. 303–15; R. M. Locke, 'The composite economy: local politics and industrial change in contemporary Italy', *Economy and Society*, 25 (1996): 483–510.

[11] D. Newlands, 'The economic role of regional governments in the European community', in S. Hardy, M. Hart, L. Albrechts, and A. Katos (eds.), *An Enlarged Europe: Regions in Competition?* London: Jessica Kingsley, 1995, pp. 70–80.

[12] For a discussion of such organizations in developing countries see the various contributions in *Firm Connections*, 4/6 (1996).

that may be cited out of the scores if not hundreds of similar entities in the United States today is *Joint Venture: Silicon Valley*. This is an extremely ambitious private–public partnership launched in 1992 with the goal of bringing together all major constituencies in Silicon Valley in an effort to secure durable agreements about its future pathway of development and to implement specific action programs in such critical areas as technology-sharing, labor training, education, assistance to small entrepreneurs, and so on.[13]

It is too early at this stage to know if the achievements of this particular organization will ever match up to its aspirations. The point, rather, is that it is representative of a profound shift in business communities in contemporary America away from simple boosterism and toward more focused and substantive forms of intervention. What is more, a good deal of this shift is based in civil organizations. No doubt, like traditional boosterism, this kind of intervention is still very much motivated by rent-seeking on the part of propertied interests and their cohorts; but it also displays a new-found awareness of and sophistication about the detailed inner workings of the local economy and how public efforts can help to deal with some of its weaker internal connections.[14]

The inter-regional dimension

Whether or not fully–fledged regional directorates eventually condense out on the economic landscape in anything even resembling the hypothetical shape outlined above, a collective consciousness of local identity and a will to act seem clearly to be on the rise in regional communities throughout the more developed parts of the world. As this trend intensifies, it is likely in turn to create new problems and predicaments *between* regions, thus calling for regulatory supervision by yet higher political authority. Among other things, once regions acquire a collective consciousness of themselves, not just as grateful

[13] *The Joint Venture Way: Lessons for Regional Rejuvenation*, San José, Calif: Joint Venture: Silicon Valley Network, 1995.

[14] Cf. P. C. Cheshire and I. R. Gordon, 'Territorial competition and the predictability of collective (in)action', *International Journal of Urban and Regional Research*, 20 (1996): 383–99; K. R. Cox and A. Wood, 'Competition and cooperation in mediating the global: the case of local economic development', *Competition and Change*, 2 (1997): 65–94; J. R. Logan and H. L. Molotch, *Urban Fortunes: The Political Economy of Place*, Berkeley and Los Angeles: University of California Press, 1987.

recipients of individual business investments, but also as critical guarantors of overall local competitive advantage and economic performance, then inter-regional relations may well become much more highly politicized than they ever have been in the past. In brief, regions throughout the world are likely to begin to confront one another more forcefully as aggregated sets of interests, thus setting in motion new political dynamics both within the global regional mosaic itself and in all probability at supra-regional levels of economic and political organization too. Should the sovereign state truly become less capable of mediating inter-regional relations in the future, much of the regulatory burden in this regard is liable to fall increasingly on supra-national or even global institutions.

A number of possible clues about the intrinsically problematical nature of this envisioned state of affairs can be deduced both from the theoretical discussions in the present book and from recent analytical work in international political economy.[15] The following seven points offer some insights into the class of problems I am referring to here, though I make no claims about their comprehensiveness. All of them represent variations on the theme of the need for authoritative political arbitration as the intensification of local social and economic organization in pursuit of competitive advantage leads to ever-increasing rivalries and clashes between regions on the world stage.

1. To begin with, we may expect to see a proliferation of economic development races between various regions, especially as increasing-returns effects give those regions that make an early start on cultivating new industries and that move fast a sharp competitive edge. A concrete example of such a race is offered by the strenuous political exertions being made in both Los Angeles and the Bay Area in California to capture the lead in the development of new multimedia industries.[16] In pursuit of first-mover advantages and other agglomeration economies, regional governments may well begin in aggregate to overinvest in particular lines of development. In this process considerable waste of resources is apt to occur unless enforceable

[15] Cf. B. Hocking, 'Regionalism: an international relations perspective', in M. Keating and J. Loughlin (eds.), *The Political Economy of Regionalism*, London: Frank Cass, 1997, pp. 90–111.

[16] A. J. Scott, 'From Silicon Valley to Hollywood: growth and development of the multimedia industry in California', in H. Braczyk, P. Cooke, and M. Heidenreich (eds.), *Regional Innovation Systems*, London: UCL Press, 1997, pp. 136–62.

inter-regional agreements about economic agendas and priorities can be hammered out. By the same token, policy should seek wherever feasible to encourage regional specialization rather than attempted duplication of economic achievements elsewhere.[17]

2. Regions that find themselves under increasing economic threat may seek to engage in protectionist maneuvers, possibly leading to further rounds of protectionism in other regions. In the USA this possibility is foreclosed by legal impediments to the restriction of inter-state commerce. In the European Union it is averted by prevailing open market rules. In a prospective global mosaic of regions, some parallel set of rules is likely to be desirable, in conjunction with appropriate safeguards to protect regions in stress.

3. Even at the present time, many regional governments in different parts of the world engage in predatory poaching forays in an effort to attract critical resources away from other regions. But when these resources have significant positive externalities for the region that is at risk, major impairment of industrial performance may ensue, leading to a net loss of average total income. Appropriate internalization of all costs and benefits associated with this process is a pre-condition of overall efficiency.

4. A growing political self-consciousness about economic issues may well induce many regions to enter into bilateral and multilateral joint ventures with one another. This trend is already well under way in the European Union, as exemplified by the Airbus Consortium and the Four Motors Program (linking together Baden–Würrtemberg, Catalonia, Lombardy, and Rhône–Alpes).[18] Regional and industrial alliances of this type can be extremely beneficial to the participants, but they can be damaging to regions that are excluded. Some wider mediation of this process may well become necessary.

5. One of the most important classes of private beneficiary of the global regional mosaic is represented by multinational (and multi-regional) corporations. These corporations, to be sure, provide numerous critical benefits because they help in significant ways to link regional economic complexes together into far-flung commodity chains; at the

[17] M. Porter, 'Competitive advantage, agglomeration economies, and regional policy', *International Regional Science Review*, 19 (1996): 85–90.

[18] P. Cooke, 'Globalization of economic organization and the emergence of regional interstate partnerships', in C. H. Williams (ed.), *The Political Geography of the New World Order*, London: Belhaven, 1993, pp. 46–58.

same time, multinational and multiregional corporations consistently seek to take advantage of varying production conditions over space by appropriate adjustments of investments and employment levels at different locations. Their concomitant ability to play regions off against one another is an issue that persistently evades effective regulation. The predicament is compounded by the demands on the public purse that large corporations often make in order to locate in any given place. This problem is actually likely to intensify in the future, because regions are much less able to resist such demands than sovereign states.

6. Long-distance migratory flows from poor to wealthy regions will almost certainly pose increasing political dilemmas for local governments, above all in cases where national frontiers are porous (cf. the current clashes between the state of California and the federal government over illegal immigration issues). How, we may ask, are sending and receiving regions to develop and enforce protocols that will eliminate the worst abuses of this process in a world where inter-regional contacts are becoming ever more free? And what effects will the transnational communities that are being brought into being in particular places by intensified migration have on conceptions of citizenship and on the construction of inter-regional alliances?

7. Perhaps most perplexing of all in this looming new world order is the gulf that will almost certainly continue to separate more-developed and less-developed regions, and that may well even become exacerbated by the various tendencies identified in these pages.[19] This observation raises difficult issues in general about inter-regional responsibilities and redistributive obligations on both a continental and a world scale, and about the types of regulatory instruments (such as the EU's Structural Funds program) that might be capable of dealing with them. This is probably the most stubbornly perplexing dilemma of all those enumerated here.

Reprise

These speculations about the escalating politicization of regional growth and development—even as the supremacy of the sovereign state is undergoing abridgement relative to its high point at mid-century—raise the double specter of intensified conflicts both within

---

[19] Cf. B. Jones, 'Conclusion', in B. Jones and M. Keating (eds.), *The European Union and the Regions*, Oxford: Clarendon Press, 1995, pp. 289–96.

and between regions. The same politicization, however, can also play a positive role by promoting the expression of ideas and aspirations about communal life that are currently submerged within social arrangements that give them little or no opportunity to become articulated over a wide front. The resurgence of regions in today's world creates a new set of political opportunities for the re-expression of political agendas at a geographic level that has hitherto always been of secondary importance, and where they are likely to be reformulated in novel forms.

It needs to be acknowledged in this regard that the continued spatial fragmentation of the world into a mosaic of regions may well, by default or social inertia, yield decisive economic and political gains to those who already enjoy disproportionate shares of wealth and power. While this possibility cannot be excluded, the analysis that I have presented, if correct, also provides a point of reference and (implicitly) a few guidelines for progressive political practices in the continuing struggle for material prosperity and democratic social conditions for all. These remarks now merit further elaboration.

COMMUNITY, LOCAL DEMOCRACY, AND CITIZENSHIP

Thus far in the discussion, I have approached the problem of the regional collectivity mainly as an assemblage of economic phenomena, and I have dealt with governance and policy issues for the most part in terms of generalized prescriptions for boosting economic performance. Regions, however, are not simply economic engines but also social communities, and these two dimensions of regional life merge with one another in elaborate and recursive relations of interdependence. The question of governance and policy, then, is intimately bound up with wider concerns, not only about the synoptic bases of economic performance, but also about income distribution and social and cultural goals. This manner of identifying the issues leads at once to the problem of how local social control is constituted, and the nature of the organizational structures through which that control is exerted. In more general terms, we may ask, what are the implications and potentialities of the governance objectives discussed here for regional political life at large?

Before any attempt is made to respond directly to this question, we need briefly to review the principal senses in which an agglomeration of producers can also be called a community. At a minimum, any agglomeration typically consists, on the one hand, of many interlocking economic activities and employment places, and on the other hand, of a working population together with dependents. The populace, moreover, is always relatively immobile.[20] These conditions of economic interdependence and human immobility in one locality can be identified as the minimal physical prerequisites of community, though they most certainly do not necessarily translate immediately into any sort of communitarian experience as such.

That said, as communities in this minimal sense come to acquire historical depth, and as social relationships are consolidated through spatial propinquity, some individuals will in all likelihood come to feel that their social identity is at least in some respects rooted in the place where they work and live. When regions are also characterized by distinctive ethnic, linguistic, or other cultural peculiarities that set them apart from other regions, their role as sources of identity and communitarian experience is usually much enhanced. In turn, and taking a cue from events in the European Union, the reinforcement of local autonomy for particular cultural groups can mitigate the sense of discrimination and administrative neglect that many of them complain bitterly about when they are subject to the authority of a strong central state, as exemplified by the cases of Catalonia, the Basque country, Brittany, Scotland, or Wales. We must, though, distinguish between the renaissance of regional identity and politics as envisioned in the present account and the atavistic regionalism evident today in parts of the former Soviet Union and Eastern Europe, which in large degree seems simply to be a reactionary expression of long-repressed ethnic grievances and hatreds.

Even at their most homogeneous, regions are in practice almost always internally divided in different ways, and they can never in any case provide an exhaustive framework of communal possibilities. In modern society, individuals are also caught up in broad webs of relationships, many of which may coincide with a particular neighborhood, region, or state, while many others find their primary definition in non-spatial (or only contingently spatial) attributes, e.g. feminists, physicists, sailing enthusiasts, stamp collectors, and so on. It is not possible, then, to assimilate the logic of contemporary regionalism

---

[20] E. Frazer, 'The value of locality', in D. King and G. Stoker (eds.), *Rethinking Local Democracy*, London: Macmillan, 1996, pp. 89–110.

into some species of pre-modern civic republicanism or Tocquevillian communitarianism (which is another reason for resisting the term 'city-state' to designate the new regional collectivities appearing on the world map at the end of the twentieth century). At the same time, and for all the reasons already adduced, regions invariably do represent identifiable if limited communities of interest, and as such they are an authentic arena of political identity and organization.

A further stimulus to the revitalization of political life in the regions of the new global mosaic is that, as they come to acquire more fully developed capacities for collective decision-making and action, contentious issues will undoubtedly multiply, both inter-regionally (e.g. over collisions of interest between different regional authorities) and intra-regionally (e.g. over issues of long-run development strategies), with some corresponding probability that levels of concern and participation on the part of those most affected will rise. Also, the fact that regions occur at a geographic scale which coincides roughly with the orbit of daily life potentially imbues all such issues with a tangibility and a relevance to the electorate that seem signally to be lacking at the present time in the arena of national politics.

A thoroughgoing regionalism, in other words, makes possible more sensitive and geographically specific kinds of governance than are ever likely to emerge when political control is concentrated in the hands of the centralized bureaucratic state. By the same token, it brings into the domain of social decidability problematical aspects of economic and social existence that evade effective adjudication under more remote systems of regulation. Regionalism is therefore fully consistent with current efforts to remobilize democratic principles in modern life, as it is also with the distinctive notion of radical democracy that Mouffe has expounded, and whose practical goals are the extension of the rights, liberties, and forms of equality propounded by the idea of liberal democracy into all the far corners of society.[21] Rights for minority language groups, welfare for immigrants, protection for those who pursue minority or unconventional life-styles, improved educational opportunities for the disadvantaged, and so on can all conceivably be dealt with more effectively by local

[21] C. Mouffe, 'Democratic citizenship and the political community', in C. Mouffe (ed.), *Dimensions of Radical Democracy*, London: Verso, 1992, pp. 225–39; C. Mouffe, 'Radical democracy or liberal democracy?' in D. Trend (ed.), *Radical Democracy: Identity, Citizenship, and the State*, New York: Routledge, 1996, pp. 19–26.

authorities than by distant state bureaucracies, and, most assuredly, attention to locally idiosyncratic details can be achieved only by appropriate decentralization.

The problem here is that there is nothing inherent in regionalism as such that necessarily promotes either the radical democratic commitments or the forms of civic virtue that are the essential underpinnings of this vision. In and of itself, the region can be a medium of regressive social policies and elite rule as much as it can be a vehicle of democratization and social participation. Yet in a world where, in the view of Holston and Appadurai, the citizens of nations are now in significant ways reduced to the role of passive spectators of the political stage, the region (or *place*, in Holston and Appadurai's terms) holds out the plausible prospect of a more immediate and personalized style of citizenship, just as it is also a fundamental unit of social affiliation.[22] Politics is no longer necessarily concentrated wholly on the business of the classical state (if it ever was), but now also concerns the negotiation of social outcomes and identities at all spatial levels from the regional to the global. Moreover, citizenship in the narrow sense (i.e. formal membership in a sovereign state) poses itself as a universal principle that in practice masks enormous inequalities and that helps to disarm critical assessment of their detailed ramifications. This is not to proclaim or prescribe an eventual evacuation of politics from constituencies above the level of the regional (i.e. the national, multinational, and global). To the contrary, these other constituencies are the sites of many urgent political dilemmas, made all the more complicated at the multinational and global levels by the intensifying imperatives of economic and social regulation at the highest as well as the lowest scales of geographic resolution.[23] My objective here is only to reaffirm the view that the current conjuncture offers many new and potentially progressive opportunities for political devolution to the regions, and for many new kinds of political engagement.

The widening consciousness of these possibilities is now evident in a re-opening of debates—especially in Europe, where these matters have a particular immediacy—about regional life and political engagement, including a clearly rising interest in associational democracy

---

[22] J. Holston and A. Appadurai, 'Cities and citizenship', *Public Culture*, 19 (1996): 187–204.

[23] P. B. Clarke, *Deep Citizenship*, London: Pluto Press, 1996.

by means of voluntary and self-governing organizations.[24] Along with these debates has come a series of efforts to reassess the notion of citizenship, so that we may conceive of it not solely as a legal birthright accorded by a sovereign state, but also as a civil attribute obtained by residency in a particular place, which carries with it substantive rights and obligations peculiar to that place. As such, citizenships would now be acquired and re-acquired many times over as individuals move from place to place over the course of their lifetimes. One immediate effect of any such reform would be the enfranchisement of the large, marginalized populations in polyglot world cities, thus opening the way for their incorporation into the political life of the community. It might perhaps even be possible to conceive of some future state of the world where individuals move from time to time, Tiebout-style, in pursuit not only of higher levels of income but also higher levels of satisfaction in relationship to the diverse social, political, and cultural amenities offered by different regions in many different parts of the world.[25]

In any case, the emerging global mosaic of regions provides an evolving terrain for numerous experiments in building new types of local political institution and forms of social conviviality, as well as new types of economic community. Putnam's hypothesis concerning the existence of a positive correlation between forms of local democratic participation and communal spirit on the one side and economic development on the other (notwithstanding the criticisms that have been levelled against his over-hasty derivation of economic dynamism out of civic culture) is of considerable interest in this context.[26] The

---

[24] See e.g. A. Amin and N. Thrift, 'Institutional issues for the European regions: from markets and plans to socioeconomics and powers of association', *Economy and Society*, 24 (1995): 41–66; S. Garcia, 'Cities and citizenship', *International Journal of Urban and Regional Research*, 20 (1996): 7–21; J. Grahl, 'Regional citizenship and macroeconomic constraints in the European Union', *International Journal of Urban and Regional Research*, 20 (1996): 480–97; P. Hirst, *Associative Democracy: New Forms of Economic and Social Governance*, Cambridge: Polity Press, 1994.

[25] C. M. Tiebout, 'The pure theory of local expenditures', *Journal of Political Economy*, 64 (1956): 416–24.

[26] R. Putnam, *Making Democracy Work: Civic Transactions in Modern Italy*, Princeton: Princeton University Press, 1993. See also: R. M. Locke, 'The composite economy: local politics and industrial change in contemporary Italy', *Economy and Society*, 25 (1996): 483–510. For critical assessments of Putnam's work see E. Goldberg, 'Thinking about how democracy works', *Politics and Society*, 24 (1996): 7–18; M. Levi, 'Social and unsocial capital: a review essay of Robert Putnam's *Making Democracy Work*', *Politics and Society*, 24 (1996): 45–53; F. Sabetti, 'Path dependency and civic culture: some lessons from Italy about interpreting social experiments', *Politics and Society*, 24 (1996): 19–44.

hypothesis, if crudely articulated and tested in its original formulation, rings true not only because active participation in local affairs, structured by institutional contexts that elicit cooperative effort and information exchange, is prone to yield more constructive results than simple withdrawal or departure (Hirschman's voice versus exit[27]), but also, as I have argued insistently in earlier chapters, because cooperation and institutional collaboration are the essential leavening of competitive advantage in modern regional economies.

[27] A. Hirschman, *Exit, Voice and Loyalty: Responses to Decline in Firms, Organizations and States*, Cambridge, Mass.: Harvard University Press, 1970.

9

The Changing Geopolitics of Production, Competition, and Regional Interdependence

For much of the twentieth century, it has been possible to trace out the geographical contours of world political economy in terms of three main systemic elements: (*a*) an evolving structure of core and peripheral areas at the international scale; (*b*) a collection of states and their corresponding national economies, forming the basic units of this structure; and (*c*) a further core–periphery dichotomy at the intranational scale. An additional tense force-field of relationships over the twentieth century has revolved around the international balance of power as represented by shifting political coalitions and animosities as well as the trade relations and economic interdependencies prevailing among sovereign states.

This complex palimpsest is still quite evident in the world today, and it will no doubt continue to persist for some considerable time to come. Equally, as I have argued insistently in all that has gone before, we seem to be poised at the threshold of a series of major transformations in this state of affairs. For one thing, the sovereign state is now much less autarchic than it once was in the economic sphere. Its former command over an identifiably national economy has been greatly reduced by the progressive globalization and de-nationalization of capital flows, production relations, information, and markets for both merchandise and services that has been occurring of late decades. Thus, at least some of the state's governance capabilities in these areas are now less assured than they once were. In addition, its coherence and powers of command are being eroded from below as a result of the re-assertion of the region as a polarized focus of economic development and by the concomitant rise of region-based modes of social regulation. Regional collectivities, moreover, are wont to seek out ever-wider margins of independent maneuver for themselves, especially in a world where the central state, as such, is less and less able to deal responsively with each region's idiosyncratic problems, needs, and aspirations, and above all when these are related in some way to wider global pressures. The net result is that a major

geopolitical shift seems now to be under way in which the old dis-
pensation, focused pre-eminently on the sovereign state and the national
economy, is receding before a new geometry of economic and political relationships, comprising a multi-level system anchored at one
end by a nexus of global interactions and at the other end by swarms
of increasingly self-assertive regions, with intermediate tiers made up
by multi-nation blocs and restructured nation states.

As I have tried to show, the ascent of a post-fordist economy based
on new information-intensive technologies and organizational capacities,
together with a conspicuous fragmentation and destabilization of
markets, has brought into being a set of conditions under which a resurgence of regional economic activity is now occurring throughout the
world. So pervasive is this resurgence that we can observe both continued vigorous growth of existing regional super-clusters and the
emergence of new major nodes of economic activity at ever more far-
flung locations. Globalization, far from undermining this process, actually intensifies its operation by extending markets for regional products
and services to the entire world, thus reinforcing the localized virtuous
circle that links together intra-regional divisions of labor, specialization, social learning, innovation, and economic growth. Simultaneously, the main geographic framework of inter-regional divisions of
labor, and hence inter-regional interdependencies, is starting to shift
from the level of the national economy to the world as a whole.

In this context, a reorientation of development strategies in economically backward countries is now both feasible and desirable by
means of a concerted focus on the region, and above all by seeking
to build appropriate economic and institutional structures in selected
regions where there is at least some chance that they can eventually
accede to a place within the global mosaic. One might say, indeed,
that the central question of classical political economy about the
wealth of nations is being transformed in today's world into another
question about the sources and the dynamics of the wealth of regions.

Regional economies function as organized entities in which the
competitive advantages and economic destiny of each individual firm
are intimately linked to the competitive advantages and economic
destiny of all local firms in aggregate. This remark implies at once
that the region is also a political entity, in the sense that its characteristic forms of work and life are indelibly inscribed in structures of
collective order. In response to this condition, a remarkable variety

of types and styles of regional economic governance arrangements is observable at the present time in many different parts of the world, though it must be added that the domain of regional governance still remains more an area of latent opportunity than it does of actual accomplishment. What is more, there does not appear to be much either in practice or in theory in the way of definitive guidelines pointing toward effective future models.

I have suggested in the previous chapter that something like a system of regional directorates may one day come into being in response to the regulatory needs and imperatives of regional economies, though I have also been deliberately guarded about their possible structural shape and substantive content. In any case, the eventual reinforcement and formalization of new structures of regional economic governance is almost certainly on the cards over the long term, for two compelling reasons. First, regions are constituted as critical collectivities of interdependent activities whose material interests are best served where certain institutionalized forms of local coordination and guidance are in place. Second, they are also increasingly vulnerable to massive stresses and strains in a world where the sovereign state is no longer always able to shelter them from the vagaries of global competition, or to mediate critically on their behalf with other regions —collaborators as well as competitors—in other parts of the world.

Finally, the revival of regions as foci of economic and political activity holds out a number of new possibilities for the remaking of communal life, and most especially for rethinking the critical contemporary issues of citizenship and democracy in the context of local society. The pressure in this direction comes in part from the very same processes that are resulting in the debordering of sovereign states. In the words of Harris,

The project of building a national state of self-governing citizens in which all have rights and duties is now part of the past . . . For the best part of thirty years, the developed states have been dismantling trade and currency regulations, capital and finance, and more recently, domestic labor markets, conditions of work and the structure of social support . . . Thus, the profound difference between citizens and foreigners upon which the socialized state was founded, is being progressively blurred.[1]

---

[1] N. Harris, *The New Untouchables: Immigration and the New World Order*, London: Penguin Books, 1995, p. 215.

Part of the pressure, as well, comes from the deeply rooted forms of demographic and political reorganization now going on in many regions, hence opening up hitherto foreclosed prospects for democratic action and the creation of local identity.

Individuals are, of course, caught up in multiple political relationships reflecting the geographic and functional complexity of modern society, and it would be a major error to seek to assimilate all of these into the ambit of the region. That said, regions are the immediate home-places of large numbers of individuals over considerable portions of their lifetime, and they also correspond roughly to the shared sphere of daily work and social existence for large groups of people. There are therefore good reasons for seeking to re-energize those civic forces of voice and social participation that are no doubt abundantly present in most regions, but that seem for the most part to lie dormant at the present time. Even though citizenship by virtue of national birthright will almost certainly continue to hold a privileged legal status for the foreseeable future, the prospect of subsidiary forms of regional citizenship on the basis of place of residence needs to be taken seriously. Citizenship of this type would confer regional rights, entitlements, and obligations on residents, enfranchising them with respect to local political processes, and helping to incorporate all those who find themselves as co-participants in a lived everyday space— no matter where they were born—into a community of interests and identity. The goal in the end is not so much the realization of some romantic vision of communal harmony, but rather a clearer and more democratic articulation of the specific political tasks that need to be accomplished at the local level relative to the new global context. Even so, the prospective rearrangement of the institutional bases of regional society encourages hopeful speculation about possible future forms of local association, sociability, and politics.

The trends identified in this book, however, have a dark as well as an auspicious side, and constant intellectual vigilance and social mobilization are essential if the latter is to triumph in the long run. A particular danger, it seems to me, is represented by currently fashionable neo-conservative policy advocacies, with their glorification of privatized, atomistic, competitive social relations and their signal and irrational aversion to anything that points in the direction of collective choice in economic matters. However, any failure in the future to set in place the institutional infrastructures needed to reap the benefits of co-operation, coordination, and strategic planning in the new global mosaic of regions is likely to result in many deepening predicaments. The viable alternative to neo-conservatism, I would argue, is a reconstructed politics of social democracy with specific organizational articulations corresponding to every geographical level of modern capitalism, from the local to the global.

INDEX

advanced economies 33, 35, 44
  see also: high-income countries,
    richer countries
Aero, A. 130
aerospace industry 64, 78
  see also: aircraft industry
Africa 70, 122, 131, 136
agglomeration 15, 63, 64, 68, 85,
    89–95, 97, 98, 100, 103, 106, 107,
    110–12, 114–16, 125, 127, 134,
    136, 140, 149, 150, 152, 153
  definition of 64–8
  forms of 89–91
  static theory of 91–4
  dynamic theory of 94–8
  in historical perspective 98–100
  and collective order 101–20
  and economic development 121–36
  see also: clustering, regional
    growth, regional motors
agglomeration
  -diseconomies 97
  -economies 63, 68, 90, 94, 95, 98,
    106, 107, 111, 114–16, 134, 136,
    149, 150
  see also: externalities, increasing
    returns
agglomeration-specific needs/skills 92,
    134
aggregate demand 103, 105
Agnew, J. 45, 70
Aglietta, M. 5
Aichi 54
Airbus Consortium 150
aircraft industry 64, 76, 95
  see also: aerospace industry
airports 92
Albert, M. 21, 22, 137
Alchian, A. A. 77
Alexander, J. W. 49
American Dream 65
Amin, A. 45, 109, 116, 156
Amin, S. 44
Amorim, M. A. 130
Amsden, A. H. 102, 128
anarchy 12
Anderson, B. 11

Anderson, P. 12
Andrews, R. B. 49
Angel, D. P. 114
APEC 10, 139
Appadurai, A. 155
Appalachia 104
Argentina 122
Arthur, W. B. 64, 95
artificial flowers 135
artisanal industry 127, 134
  see also: craft manufacturing,
    post-fordist industry
ASEAN 10
Asia 3, 28, 44, 65, 67, 70, 100, 117,
    122, 128, 131, 139, 140
  see also: East Asia, South-east Asia
assembly line 18
  see also: mass production, fordism,
    fordist mass production
associational democracy 155
atavistic regionalism 153
athletic shoes 40, 135
Austin, TX. 67
Australia 122, 123

backward regions 7
  see also: less developed regions,
    poor regions, underdeveloped areas
backwash 43
Baden-Würrtemberg 146, 150
Badie, B. 45
Balassa, B. 125
Baltic Republics 123
Bangalore 128
Bangkok 70, 110, 128
Barro, R. J. 105
basic and non-basic production 49
Basque Country 153
Bay Area Multimedia Partnership 113
Becattini, G. 86, 108
Beijing 121
Belgian confederate system 147
Belgium 121
Bennett, R, J. 146
Best, M. H. 114, 115
Bianchi, P. 147
billiard ball analogy 9, 25

biotechnology industry 93
Birmingham 99
Blackley, P. R. 61
Bluestone, B. 61
blue-collar workers 18
    see also: production workers,
        working class
Böhm-Bawerck, E. von 76
Bombay 121, 124
boosterism 115, 148
Boston 68, 120
bottom up development 103, 146
Bourguinat, H. 10
Boyer, R. 5, 103
Bozorgmehr, M. 72
branch plants 28, 36, 44, 71, 128
    see also: multinational corporations
branching process 114
    see also: path dependency
Brasilia 2
Brazil 5, 28, 105, 122, 123, 128, 130,
    131, 135
breakthrough moment 95
Bretton Woods 27
Britain 13, 14, 16, 17, 21, 99, 104,
    106, 115, 142
Brittany 153
Brock, L. 22
Brown, D. 113
Brusco, S. 113
Brussels 147
Buenos Aires 121
Burgess, E. W. 99
business
    -conventions 90
    -cycle 38

Calcutta 121
California 2, 64, 65, 92, 147–9, 151
    see also: Bay Area, Southern
        California, Los Angeles
Cambodia 122
Camilleri, J. A. 41
Canada 104, 122, 123, 142
capital
    -accumulation 12, 14
    -cities 48
capitalism 5, 6, 9, 11–17, 19, 21, 23,
    25, 26, 42–5, 47, 49, 70, 98,
    100–2, 121, 125, 130, 140–2, 163
    in historical perspective 9–24

from internationalization to
    globalization 25–46
    and the new world order 159–64
capitalist development 14, 21, 48, 54,
    66
capital
    -intensive products 44
    -labor ratio 59, 61, 62
Caracas 124
CARICOM 10
Carlton, D. W. 77
carpentry 13
car industry 18, 21, 65, 82, 95
Carter presidency 20
Cassa per il Mezzogiorno 104
Castells, M. 70, 107
Catalonia 150, 153
Cawthorne, P. 130
Census of Manufactures 62
Central America 72
Central Scotland 104
central-place systems 88
ceramics industry 129
chaebol 128
Champagne 109
Chandler, A. D. 18
Channel Tunnel 146
Chenery, H. B. 105
Cheshire, P. C. 148
Chicago 54, 57, 65, 85, 99
China 3, 5, 123
Christaller, W. 85
Christopherson, S. 64
citizenship 6, 11, 142, 151, 152,
    154–6, 161, 162
    and local democracy 152–8
City of London 108, 109
city-state 144, 154
    see also: regional directorates
civic republicanism 154
civil
    -organizations 104, 147, 148
        see also: institutions
    -rights 41
    -society 5, 6
Clarke, P. B. 155
classical
    -location theory
        see: location theory
    -state 5, 10, 12, 23, 155
        see also: state apparatus

clothing industry 62
  see also: garment industry, fashion
    clothing, *haute couture*
clustering 48, 49, 57, 61–3, 127
  see also: agglomeration
Coase, R. H. 76, 77
Coca Cola 40
Cold War 20, 28
collaborative networks 112, 119, 134
collective
  -consciousness 148
  -decision-making and behavior 103
  -order 6, 101, 102, 106, 119, 124,
    143, 160
  see also: governance, institutions
colleges and universities 112
Committee of the Regions 141
commodity chains 28, 47, 68, 135, 150
community
  and collective action 101–3
  and local democracy 152–64
  see also: regional directorate,
    Tocquevillian communitarianism
comparative advantage 43, 45, 65
  see also competitive advantage
competition and collaboration 7, 82,
  143
competitive advantage 3, 7, 45, 48, 61,
  64, 94, 97, 103, 107, 108, 111,
  114, 116, 117, 120, 123, 130, 134,
  143, 149, 150, 157, 160
  analytics of 75–100
  social construction of 101–20
  in backward regions 137–58
competitive performance 134
Congress of Vienna 11
consumer goods 53
conventions 6, 41, 82, 90, 97, 101,
  107, 108, 124, 139
  see also: institutions, cultural
    routines
Cooke, P. 86, 112, 120, 146, 149, 150
coordinating mechanisms 111
Corbridge, S. 45, 70, 108, 133
core countries 71
core-periphery 14, 43, 44, 66, 159
Coriat, B. 100
corporate organization 101
cost-cutting 110
Côte, M. 116
cotton knitwear 130

country prejudices 93
Cox, K. R. 148
craft manufacturing 94, 131
  see also: post-fordist industry, Third
    Italy
cultural
  -routines 91
  -products industries 53, 94, 109, 119
  -factors in social regulation 107–16
  see also: conventions
cutlery industry 99
cut-throat competition 108
Cyberjaya 2

Danish furniture 109
David, P. A. 64, 97
Dawson, J. 130
DC-3 aircraft 95
debordering 21, 22, 161
democracy 6, 11, 109, 120, 141,
  152–6, 161, 163
  local democracy and citizenship
    152–8
  see also: associational democracy,
    citizenship
democratic ideals and principles 13,
  141, 154
Demsetz, H. 77
Denmark 116
Department of Economic Affairs 104
Department of Regional Economic
  Expansion 104
design services 111
deskilling 61
Detroit 40, 57, 64, 65, 95
Deudney, D. 41
developmental paths and trajectories
  114, 115
  see also: path dependency
De Vet, J. M. 90
division of labor 5, 7, 15, 16, 18, 33,
  44, 45, 54, 70, 71, 76–8, 81, 83,
  91, 92, 95, 97, 123, 127, 128,
  130
  and the theory of location 91–8
  see also: new international division
    of labor, social division of
    labor, technical division of
    labor
domestic appliances 18, 65
Douglas, D. 95

dynamic
-learning effects 97
  see also: innovation, learning
    economy
-vertical disintegration 95
  see also: vertical disintegration
dysfunctional attitudes 110

early start 97, 98, 114, 149
  see also: first mover advantages
East and South-east Asia 28, 140
  see also: South-east Asia
Eastern Europe 153
economic
-backwardness 122
  see also: poor regions, less
    developed areas, Third World
-development 13, 16, 41, 43, 64, 70,
  75, 104, 106, 107, 109, 113, 115,
  121, 124, 125, 128, 129, 133, 135,
  136, 146–9, 156, 159
-development races 149
-geography 6, 7, 13, 45, 49, 54, 62,
  67, 68, 85, 86, 89, 90, 137
-performance 75, 102, 107, 149, 152
  regional bases of 75–6
-space 76, 78, 81–3, 91
  see also: geographic space
-theory 75, 102
Economic Development Administration
  104
economies
-of scale 18, 33, 65, 83, 97, 105,
  111, 125, 139
  see also: internal economies of
    scale
-of scope 77, 84
Ecuador 130
eighteenth century 15, 25
electric cars 82
electronic
-communications systems 40
-components 100
electro-mechanical technologies 129
Emmanuel, A. 44
employment places 92, 153
end of the Third World 121, 123
entrepôts 129
entrepreneurship 111, 115
entropy 4, 88
establishment size 62, 63, 117

Europe 3, 7, 12–14, 18, 20, 22, 28, 29,
  33, 43, 44, 63, 65, 66, 70, 100,
  104, 106, 111, 121, 140, 146, 147,
  153, 155
  see also: Western Europe
European Union (EU) 10, 42, 71, 139,
  141, 146, 150, 151, 153, 156
exchange rates 27, 125, 139
export
-promotion 136
-oriented growth/industrialization 33,
  71, 122, 123
expressways 92
extensive margins of capitalism 48, 121
externalities 81, 83, 86, 88–91, 103,
  107, 119, 143, 150
  see also: agglomeration economies,
    economies of scale, economies of
    scope, increasing returns
extra-local transactions 89

face-to-face encounters 84, 89
Fairchild Semiconductor 95
Falk, J. 41
FAO 41
fashion clothing 53, 100
  see also: haute couture
FDI 36, 38
feminists 153
feudalism 11
fiduciary guarantees 108
film industry 21, 53, 64, 82, 88, 100,
  109, 110
  see also: Hollywood
financial
-crisis 38
-services 82, 100, 108, 109
Firm Connections 147
first-mover advantages 114, 135, 147,
  149
  see also: early start
First World 44
fiscal incentives 116
Flanders 16, 146, 147
flexible
-production 22, 67, 89, 94, 100
-specialization 64, 129, 130, 146
  see also: craft, industry, post-
    fordist industry
Florentine leather goods 109
Florida, R. 67, 93

footwear industry
  see: shoe industry
Ford, H. 95
fordism 18–24, 28, 100, 103, 106
fordist mass production 19–21, 65, 66,
  99, 100, 105, 129
  see also: mass production
foreign
  -affiliates 36, 38
    see also: branch plants,
      multinational corporations
  -aid 125
  -direct investment 10, 36
  -exchange 27, 28, 38
  -trade 26, 29, 38, 40, 57
forestry 122
Fortune Global 500 36
Fos-sur-Mer 105
Four Motors of Europe Program 150
France 4, 12, 16, 36, 76, 82, 104, 105,
  112, 121, 146, 147
Frank, A. G. 43, 44, 149
Frankfurt 57, 67
Frazer, E. 153
free trade 16, 17, 28, 139
  see also: laisser-faire
Friedman, J. 72
Friedman, D. B. 108
Fröbel, F. 44
Frostbelt 67
  see also: Manufacturing Belt
furniture industry 100, 109, 113, 115,
  117, 119, 129, 130
Furniture New York 113

G7 41
Gabon 123
Garcia, S. 156
garment industry 130
  see also: clothing industry, fashion
    clothing, *haute couture*
GATT 27
GDP 25, 26, 29, 33, 35, 36, 38, 40,
  123, 125
gem-cutting 110
  see also: jewelry industry
Genoa 68
geographic change 21
geographic space 14, 43, 48, 78, 83,
  85, 91, 121
  see also: economic space

geographical disparities 146
  see also: unequal development
geopolitics 41, 159
Gereffi, G. 47, 135
German states 17
Germany 5, 16, 17, 36, 65, 85, 142
Ghana 130
Gilpin, R. 27
global
  -competition 114, 161
  -economy 22, 45, 68, 72, 86, 90,
    100, 136, 144
    see also: new international division
      of labor
  -hierarchy of governance relations
    138–40
  -mosaic of regions 6, 7, 47, 48, 123,
    140, 143, 150, 154, 156, 160, 163
  -reach 53
globalism 20–3
globalization 1, 4, 21, 22, 25–8, 36, 40,
  42, 44, 45, 47, 48, 67, 71, 72, 90,
  100, 106, 123, 135, 139, 142, 150,
  159, 160
  subsequent to internationalization
    25–46
  regional expressions of 47–74
  and regional politics 137–58
  geopolitics of 159–64
gold standard 27, 28
Goldberg, E. 156
Golden Age of capitalism 19
Gordenker, L. 42
Gordon, I. R. 148
governance 5–7, 12, 41, 42, 46, 102–4,
  112, 137, 139–42, 144, 146, 147,
  152, 154, 156, 159, 161
  collective order and regional
    development 101–20
  in the global regional mosaic 137–58
    see also: institutions
governmental agencies/bureaucracies
  101, 103, 120, 144
Grahl, J. 156
Granovetter, M. 78
Great Depression 104
Great Lakes 14
Greytak, D. 61
growth centers 66, 105
  see also: agglomeration, geographic
    space

growth poles 18, 20, 105
  see also: economic space
Guangzhou 70
Guéhenno, J-M. 140

habituation 92
  see also: socialization
Haitians 72
Hall, P. 107
Hansen, N. 105
Harris, N. 123, 127, 161
Harrison, B. 61, 75
haute couture 109
  see also: clothing industry, fashion
  clothing, garment industry
heartlands 121
Heckscher-Ohlin theory 16
Hegel, G. F. W. 11
Heinrichs, J. 44
Held, D. 141
Henderson, J. 44, 128
Henderson, J. V. 53
Herrigel, G. 146
Higgins, B. 105
High Fordism 100
high-income countries 125, 127
  see also: richer countries
high-technology industry 64, 106,
  107
Hirschman, A. 43, 45, 136, 157
Hirst, P. 26, 115, 156
Hobbes 11
Hocking, B. 149
Holland 121
Hollywood 3, 40, 88, 109, 110, 149
Holston, J. 155
homeworkers 130
Hong Kong 70–2, 122, 123, 129, 135,
  146
horizontal cooperation 131
  see also: collaborative networks
Hoselitz, B. 133
Hounshell, D. A. 66
housing 111
Houston 57
Hungary 123
hysteresis 43, 64

illegal immigration 151
ILO 41
imagined community 11
  see also: nation-state

IMF 27, 38, 41, 136
import substitution 105, 122, 123, 128,
  134, 136
Inchon 128
increasing returns 33, 64, 68, 76, 81,
  86, 92, 94, 97, 98, 127, 134, 135,
  144, 149
  and regional growth 75–100
  social and political foundations of
  101–20
  see also: agglomeration economies,
  economies of scale, economies
  of scope, externalities
India 3, 70, 128, 130
Indonesia 70
industrial
  -atmosphere 83, 97
  -capitalism 5, 13, 16, 25
  -complex 95
  see also: agglomeration, economic
  space, growth poles
  -districts 82, 99, 100, 108, 110, 130,
  131
  see also: agglomeration
  -organization 62, 76–8, 117
  see also: vertical disintegration,
  vertical integration
industrialization 13, 14, 16, 17, 22, 65,
  68, 99, 100, 102–5, 108, 121, 122,
  124, 125, 128, 130, 131, 147
infant industry 95, 98, 135
infrastructural artifacts 92
Inland Sea 121
innovation 66, 75, 82, 93, 94, 97, 112,
  147, 149, 160
  see also: dynamic learning effects,
  learning economy
input-output 53, 76, 78, 81, 88
institutional thickness 109, 110
institutions 6, 12, 27, 41, 42, 101–4,
  107, 112, 114, 116, 119, 124, 131,
  144, 149
  and regional development 101–20
  and social regulation 107–16
  in the global mosaic of regions
  137–58
  see also: civil organizations,
  governance
institution-building 103, 106, 116, 134
intellectual property rights 139
internal economies of scale 18, 65
  see also: economies of scale

international
  -associations 41
  -political economy 16, 45, 70, 128,
    149
  -trade 15, 20, 25, 27, 29, 36, 40, 44,
    45, 57, 90
  -development agencies 122
International Bank for Reconstruction
  and Development 27
International Monetary Fund 27, 38,
  136
inter-firm
  -collaboration 117
    see also: collaborative networks
  -flows 83
    see also: linkages, transactional
      relationships inter-regional
  -agreements 150
  -trade 15
Ireland 123
Isard, W. 76, 85
Isserman, A. M. 106
Ivory Coast 70

Jakarta 124
Japan 3, 5, 27–9, 36, 44, 54, 65, 70,
  106, 108, 111, 121, 142
Japan Statistical Yearbook 54
Japanese manufacturers 20
jewelry industry 53, 78, 110
  see also: gem-cutting
jewelry design 110
Joint Venture Silicon Valley 113,
  148
joint ventures 10, 77, 104, 150
Jones, B. 146, 151
just-in-time production 4, 84

Kaldor, N. 94, 127
Kanagawa 54
kanban system 91, 104
Katzenstein, P. J. 33
Keating, M. 7, 146, 149, 151
Keen, D. 122
keiretsu 77, 108
Keohane, R. O. 41
keynesianism 21, 28
Khmer Rouge 122
kitchen utensils industry 129
know-how 64, 77, 100, 107, 108,
  128
  see also: learning economy

Korzeniewicz, M. 47
Krasner, S. D. 25
Krebs, G. 146
Kreye, O. 44
Krugman, P. 26, 33, 71
Kuala Lumpur 2, 3, 70, 128
Kumasi 130

labor market 40, 68, 78, 91, 92, 97,
  106, 109, 143, 144, 161
  see also: local labor market
labor unions 104, 112
labor-intensive production 44, 91
Lagos 124
laisser-faire 13, 17, 102
Lampard, E. E. 107
Lancashire 94, 99
land use 111
länder 146
Latin America 44, 70, 117, 122, 128,
  131
Lawrence, R. Z. 40
Lawson, V. 130
lead plants 18, 78, 99
  see also: growth poles, mass
    production
learning economy 128, 134
  see also: dynamic learning effects
leather industry 64, 109, 131, 135
Leborgne, D. 103
Lega Nord 147
legal system 101
Leonardi, R. 120
Leontieff, W. 76
less developed countries 48, 105, 127,
  131, 133, 135
  see also: low-income countries, Third
    World
Levi-Faur, D. 16
Levi, M. 156
Lewis, A. 135
liberal democracy 154
  see also: citizenship, democracy
libertarian fantasies 102
lighting technicians 109
Lille 146
linkages 18, 47, 88
  see also: face-to-face encounters,
    transactional relationships
Lipietz, A. 5, 103
liquid capital 38
List, F. 16–17

local
　-cultures 93, 109
　　and their effects on economic
　　　development 101–16
　-democracy 152, 153
　-economy 53, 111, 134, 143, 144,
　　147, 148
　　see also: agglomeration, industrial
　　　district, regional development,
　　　regional motors
　-government 7, 108, 113, 116, 142,
　　143, 147, 151
　　see also: institutions, regional
　　　directorates
　-labor market 63, 92, 124, 127
　　and agglomeration processes 92
　　see also: labor market
location theory 75, 85–91
locational decision-making 85
Locke, R. M. 22, 147, 156
Logan, J. R. 148
logistic regression 59, 61–3, 125
Lombardy 150
London 4, 57, 67, 108, 109, 115
London theater 109
Lorenz, E. H. 108
Lorraine 121
Los Angeles 54, 57, 62, 68, 72, 73, 95,
　　109, 110, 115, 117, 119, 129, 148,
　　149
　see also: Southern California
Lösch, A. 85
Löschian-Weberian landscapes 88
low-income countries 125, 127, 135
　see also: less developed countries,
　　Third world
low-wage jobs 72
Luxembourg 29

Maastricht Treaty 141
magic carpets 85, 86
Mahathir bin Mohamad, Dr. 2
Makambako 130
Malaysia 2, 105, 123, 135
managerial practices 101
Manchester 64, 124, 135
Manila 128
Mann, M. 9, 10
Manufacturing Belt 65, 99
　see also: Frostbelt
manufacturing cities 18
　see also: growth centers

Marglin, S. A. 19
market failure 6, 81, 102, 111, 112,
　　142
Marshall, A. 28, 83, 107
Marshall Plan 28
mass production 18–21, 65, 66, 99,
　　100, 105, 129
　see also: fordist mass production
Mauritius 123
Mauroy, P. 146
McKenzie, R. D. 99
medium-sized countries 40
　see also: middle-income countries
mercantilism 14, 25
MERCOSUR 10
metal
　-trades 99
　-working 15, 130
metropolis-hinterland system 68
metropolitan areas 47–9, 54, 57, 59, 62,
　　67, 99, 121, 145, 147
　world distribution of 48–52
Mexico 28, 41, 70, 105, 121, 123, 135
Mexico City 121, 122
Miami 57
Michigan 147
microelectronics industry 112
Middle East 3
middle-income countries 123, 125, 127,
　　128, 130, 133
Midlands 121
Midwest 14, 67
migration 49, 72, 124, 151
Milan 68
military spending 20
Miller, R-E. 116
million city 48
Minneapolis 57
minority language groups 154
Mittelman, J. H. 139
Molotch, H. L. 148
monetary transactions 38
Morales, R. 86
Morgan, K. 112, 146
mosaic of regions 1, 6, 47–74, 150,
　　152, 156, 163
　see also: regional motors
Mouffe, C. 154
multidivisional corporation 18
multimedia industry 2, 3, 53, 113,
　　149
Multimedia Super Corridor 2, 3

multinational corporations 36, 38, 44, 71, 128, 139
  see also: branch plants
multi-nation blocs 10, 139–41, 160
  see also: plurinational alliances
music industry 53, 109
Myrdal, G. 43, 45

Nadvi, K. 131
NAFTA 10, 139
Nagoya 68, 121
Nanetti, R. Y. 120
Napoleonic Wars 11
Nashville 109
nation state 9–20
  see also: sovereign state
national identity 142
National Shoe Fair 131
natural
  -endowments 43, 63–5, 125
    see also: comparative advantage
  -harbors 63
Nelson, R. R. 94
neoclassical economics 101
neo
  -conservatism 106, 162, 163
  -Listian policy 17, 45, 103
network brokering 115
new
  -economic geography 85
  -grammar of space 45
  -industrial spaces 22, 66, 105
  -international division of labor 44, 45, 71
  -political spaces 137–42
New Deal 19
New England 14, 64
New York 4, 14, 54, 57, 62, 67, 68, 72, 73, 113, 147
New York State Department of Economic Development 113
New Zealand 40, 122
Newlands, D. 147
newly industrializing countries 28, 70, 106, 123, 125
Nigeria 70
Nike athletic shoes 40
nineteenth century 13–15, 17, 25, 26, 63, 94, 99, 100, 124
Nixon, R. 28
non-governmental agencies 120
  see also: institutions

Nord-Pas-de-Calais 146
norms 6, 70, 101
North, D. C. 124
North America 13, 18, 20, 22, 28, 29, 43, 44, 63, 65, 66, 100, 104, 106, 111, 140
  see also: Canada, United States
Northern England 104
Northern European Plain 14
not-for-profit associations 104
Novo Hamburgo 131

O'Brian, R. 1
OECD 29, 33, 35, 36, 38, 40, 41
Ohmae, K. 5, 46, 144
oil shocks 28
Orange County, CA. 67, 93
organizational infrastructures 103
  see also: institutions
Osaka 54, 68, 121
Osborne, D. 120

Pacific Ocean 3
Pacific Rim 3
Panzar, J. C. 77
parent companies 36
  see also: multinational corporations
Paris 67, 72
Park, R. E. 99
path-dependency 86, 91, 114, 157
  see also: branching processes
Pax Americana 28
Peck, J. 92
Penang 128
Pennsylvania 147
periphery 14, 43, 44, 66, 71, 100, 104, 122, 159
  see also: core-periphery
Perroux, F. 76
Peru 130, 131
petroleum refining 18
Philadelphia 68
photographic processing 88
physicists 153
Piore, M. J. 100, 129
Pittsburgh 40
plastic footwear industry 135
plurinational alliances 42
  see also: multi-nation blocs
Poland 16, 123
Polanyi, K. 12, 101

polarization 1, 43, 122
   see also: growth poles
polarization reversal 122
political
   -boundaries 47
   -mobilization 7, 110, 134, 137
Pollard, S. 121
poor regions 121–36
   see also: backward regions
Porter, M. 64, 150
Portugal 16, 123
post-fordist industry 66, 68, 99
   see also: flexible production, flexible
     specialization
Powell, W. W. 77
pricing system 81
printed circuit boards 135
private-public partnerships 6, 104, 144
product cycle 105
production
   -function 81
   -systems 22, 36, 62, 77, 83, 84,
     89–91, 94, 100, 106, 123, 127,
     134, 135
   regional production systems 75–100
   -workers 59, 61–3
     see also: blue-collar workers
property ownership 101
protectionism 15, 25, 150
Pryke, M. 108
public health 13, 142
publishing industry 53, 59
Puerto Ricans 72
Putnam, R. D. 109, 156

Quito 130

Randstad 68
reaganism 21, 106
real services 113
Rebuild LA 115
Redfield, R. 129
redistributive programs 104
regional
   -communities 148
   -cultures 107, 109
   -development
     see: regional growth
   -development policy 116–21
     see also: regional planning
   -directorates 142, 145, 146, 148,
     161

-growth 15, 105, 131, 151
   see also: agglomeration
-marketing 113
-motors (of the global economy) 45,
   68, 72, 90, 100, 145
   see also: mosaic of regions
-planning 104, 105, 111, 116, 142
-science 85, 106, 122, 150
regionalism 36, 139, 146, 149, 153–5
regulationist theory 5, 102
   see also: institutions, social
     regulation
regulatory imperative 101
reprivatization 21
reputation effects 64, 108
resource extraction 14, 122
Rhône-Alpes 150
Ricardo, D. 15–17
Richardson, H. 122
richer countries 49
   see also: high-income countries
Rigby, D. L. 19
Rio Grande do Sul 131
robotics industry 112
Romer, P. M. 64, 94
Rondinelli, D. 122
Rosecrance, R. 22, 42
roundaboutness 76
Ruhr 121
rural areas 49, 131
Russia 123
Russo 82

Sabel, C. F. 100, 129
Sabetti, F. 156
sailing enthusiasts 153
Saillard, Y. 103
Saitama 54
Salais, R. 82
Sala-i-Martin, X. 105
San Diego 68, 93
San Francisco 57
San Jose 57, 148
Santa Clara County 114
São João do Aruaru 130
São Paulo 70, 121, 122, 128
Sassen, S. 72
Savoie, D. J. 105
Saxenian, A. 75
scale effects 33, 100
   see also: economies of scale
scenario writing 88

Schmandt, J. 106
Schmitz, H. 131–2
Schor, J. B. 19
scientific
  -congresses 90
  -research 41
Scott, A. J. 5, 22, 45, 53, 61, 62, 64,
  65, 75, 86, 92, 103, 108, 110, 114,
  115, 128, 142, 147, 149
Seattle 57, 64
Second World 104, 124
self-governing organizations 156
semiconductor industry 76, 78, 94, 95,
  114, 115, 128
Seoul 70, 121, 122, 128
services 21, 29, 36, 40, 53, 54, 63, 67,
  82, 85, 90, 92, 94, 100, 108, 109,
  111–13, 119, 127, 142, 143, 147,
  159, 160
  see also: financial services
Shanghai 121
Sheffield 99
shoe industry 40, 64, 131, 135
Silesia 121
Silicon Valley 3, 40, 64, 67, 75, 94,
  97, 113–16, 148, 149
Singapore 40, 70, 71, 122, 123, 129,
  135, 146
Singer, M. B. 129
small economic systems 33
Smith, A. 15–17
social
  -division of labor 15, 76–8, 81, 91,
    95, 97, 127, 130
    see also: technical division of
      labor, vertical disintegration
  -inertia 152
  -infrastructures 102, 109, 130, 134
    see also: institutions
  -participation 155, 162
  -regulation 5, 6, 92, 111, 116, 137,
    144, 155, 159
    see also: regulation theory
  -segmentation 72
socialization 93, 101, 107
  see also: habituation
Soja, E. W. 86
Sony Walkman 40
South Korea 102, 123, 128, 131,
  135
Southern California 64, 65
  see also: California, Los Angeles

south-east Asia 28, 140
  see also: east and south-east Asia
sovereign state 4, 6, 9–12, 22, 25, 46,
  47, 140–3, 149, 151, 155, 156,
  159–61
  see also: nation state
sovereignty 9, 25, 41, 42, 142
Soviet Union 28, 122, 136, 153
Spain 123, 135, 147
Späth, B. 128, 131
spatial concentration 54, 121, 125
  see also: agglomeration, growth
    centers, polarization
special effects industry 88
spill-overs 81
  see also: externalities, market failure
spin off 15
spinning 64, 77
stage of economic development 125
Stallings, B. 124, 135
stamp collectors 153
Stanford University 115, 141
state
  -apparatus 5, 10
  -bureaucracies 155
    see also: city-state, nation-state,
      sovereign state
static transactional theory (of location)
  91–4
steel 18
Stein, H. 136
Steinbeis Foundation 112
Stigler, G. J. 15
Storper, M. 5, 45, 64, 75, 82, 86, 90,
  103, 108, 128, 147
strategies of regional development
  116–20
strategic choice and planning 104, 107,
  114, 120, 162
Structural Funds 151
Sturt, G. 93
subcontracting 130, 143
Sunbelt 65, 67
super-clusters 89, 90, 160
  see also: regional motors
sweatshop manufacturing 72
Sweden 4
Swiss watches 109
Switzerland 41

Taiwan 40, 70, 135, 146
take-off 129

Tanzania 130
tariff barriers 17, 38, 71
tax holidays 116
technical division of labor 15, 18
  see also: social division of labor
technological
  -innovation
    see: innovation, learning economy
  -knowledge 111
    see also: know-how
  -progress 66
technology
  -systems 103
  -transfer 112
Technopolis Program 2
Teece, D. J. 77
television 21, 53
temporal steering 114
territorial state 11, 13, 22, 140
  see also: nation-state, trading state
territory 5, 11–13, 45, 48, 70, 75
textile industry 15
Thai silks 109
thatcherism 21, 106
Third Italy 108, 113, 129, 131
Third World 44, 105, 117, 121, 123,
  124, 127–9, 135
  regional development in 121–36
Thirty Years War 11
Thomas, D. 116
Thompson, G. 26
Thompson, J. E. 25
Thompson, E. P. 145
Thrift, N. 45, 108, 109, 156
Tianjin 121
Tiebout, C. M. 156
Tijuana 68
Tiruppur 130
Tocquevillian communitarianism
  154
Todaro, M. F. 124
Tokyo 54, 57, 67, 68, 72, 121
Townroe, P. M. 122
toy industry 129
trade
  -associations 112
  -fairs 90
trademarking 113
trading state 22, 42
traffic congestion 142
training centers and institutions 103,
  110, 112, 131

transactional relationships 86, 91
  see also: linkages
transactions
  -costs 78, 84, 86, 88–90
  and the theory of agglomeration
    91–7
  -intensive networks 127
transport costs 88
transportation and communication
  technologies 3, 40, 47
trans-border regions 140
  see also: tri-national region
travel time 84
Treaty of Westphalia 11
Triad countries 29, 70
trickle down 43
tri-national region 146
Trujillo 131
trust 78, 108, 110
Turin 68

Ukraine 123
umbrella organization 120
UNCTAD 38, 41
underdeveloped areas 70, 123
  see also: less developed regions
unequal
  -development 44, 122
  -exchange 44
Union of International Associations 41
United Kingdom 36, 123
United Nations 10, 27, 29, 35, 38, 41,
  42, 48
United States 5, 14, 19–21, 28, 36, 40,
  54, 57, 63, 65, 67, 70, 71, 73, 99,
  104, 106, 114, 122, 128, 142, 147,
  148
  see also: North America
upstream industries 18
urban
  -areas 4, 48, 49, 125
    see also: industrial districts,
      metropolitan areas
  -planning 13
urbanization 4, 14, 47, 48, 121, 122,
  124, 125, 127
US Department of Commerce 57

value-added networks 15, 106, 112
vehicle repair 130
Venables, A. J. 71
Vernon, R. 36

vertical disintegration 77, 89, 94, 95, 131
  conditions underlying 76
  and locational agglomeration 91–100
    see also: dynamic vertical disintegration, industrial organization, social division of labor
vertical integration 77, 78
Vietnam 70
Villarán, F. 130, 131
voice versus exit 157
von Hippel, E. 81, 82

Wade, R. 26, 102
Wagner Act 19
Waldinger, R. 72
Walker, R. 75
Wallerstein, I. 14, 43
Wallonia 147
Waltz, K. N. 9, 12
weaving 64, 77
Webber, M. J. 19
Weber, A. 41, 85
Weber, A. F. 14
Weiss, T. G. 42
welfare-statism 21
  see also: keynesianism
West Africans 72

Western Europe 7, 12–14, 18, 20, 22, 28, 29, 43, 44, 65, 66, 100, 104, 106, 111, 121, 140
  see also: Europe
Williamson, O. E. 76, 77
Willig, R. D. 77
Wilson, R. 106
window of locational opportunity 66
Winter, S. G. 94
Wolff, G. 72, 86
Wood, A. 148
woodworking industry 130
woollens 99
working class 66, 99, 145
  see also: blue-collar workers, production workers
world
  -economy 1, 14, 36, 67, 123, 125, 137
    see also: globalization, global mosaic of regions, new international division of labor
  -trade 25, 27–9, 131
World Bank 27, 41, 123, 135, 136
World Trade Organization 27
World War 2, 20, 27, 66, 123

Yorkshire 99
Young, A. 76

Zollverein 17